Lao for Beginners

by
Buasawan Simmala
(ບົວສະຫວັນ ສິມມາລາ)
and
Benjawan Poomsan Becker
(ເບັນຈະວັນ ພູມແສນ ເບັກເກີຣ໌)

PAIBOON

PUBLISHING

ພາສາລາວ

Paiboon Poomsan Publishing
582 Amarinniwate Village 2
Sukhapiban Road 1, Bungkum
Bangkok 10230
THAILAND
☎ 662-509-8632
Fax 662-519-5437

Paiboon Publishing
PMB 256, 1442A Walnut Street
Berkeley, California USA 94709
☎ 1-510-848-7086
Fax 1-510-848-4521
Email: books@paiboonpublishing.com
www.paiboonpublishing.com

สำนักพิมพ์ไพบูลย์ภูมิแสน
582 หมู่บ้านอัมรินทร์นิเวศน์ 2
ถ. สุขาภิบาล 1 เขตบึงกุ่ม
ก.ท.ม. 10230
☎ 662-509-8632
โทรสาร 662-519-5437

Email: books@paiboonpublishing.com
www.paiboonpublishing.com

Cover and graphic design by Randy Kincaid

Cover picture: Laotian woman in front of That Luang

Edited by Oun Khamvanhthong, Kamontip Topanya and Craig Becker

Voice Talent: Craig Becker, Buasawan Simmala, Johnathon Jamison, Saikham Jamison, Oun Khamvanhthong and Bouaphet Sygnavong

ISBN 1-887521-28-3

Introduction

Lao for Beginners is designed both for people who are just starting to study the Lao language for the first time and for those who want to improve their basic Lao. It teaches all four basic language skills—speaking, listening (when used with the audio), reading and writing. The first part of each lesson teaches vocabulary and sentence structure and includes a vocabulary list with Lao spelling, transliteration and definitions in English.

The transliteration system assists you with pronunciation while you are learning the Lao alphabet. It's important that you learn to properly pronounce the tones and sounds of Lao. Although *Lao for Beginners* is written with self-study in mind, as well as classroom use, a Lao teacher or tutor should listen to and correct your pronunciation, especially at the beginning.

We encourage beginning students of Lao to learn the alphabet. Even though conversation may be your principal goal, the Lao alphabet is almost 100% phonetic and studying it will reinforce speaking and listening skills as well as reading and writing. Wean yourself off of transliteration as soon as possible. You won't regret the extra effort spent learning the Lao writing system.

The second part of each lesson teaches basic reading and writing of the Lao language. It provides a guided step by step introduction to the consonants, vowels, tone rules, and other features of the written language.

Written Lao uses no spaces between words. In this text, however, we usually separate the words with a space to help you get started reading the Lao script more quickly.

The appendix features a section with useful words and phrases that you can use as a quick reference to start using some Lao right away with minimal effort.

Characteristics of the Lao language different from English include:

* There are no variant or plural forms for adjectives and nouns.

* Adjectives follow the noun.
  In Lao we say "car white" (lot sǐi kǎao) instead of "white car".

* There are no verb conjugations in Lao. We understand tenses from the context or from adverbs of time.

* There are no articles (a, an, the).

* There is no verb 'to be' with adjectives.
  "You're beautiful" would be "You beautiful" (jâo ngáam).

* There are ending particles that imply the needs and feelings of the speaker.

* Classifiers are used with virtually all nouns.

* Lao usually omits the subject of a sentence when it is understood from the context.

* Lao is a tonal language.
  If the tone is not correct, you won't be easily understood, even if your pronunciation is otherwise perfect.

* Lao is almost 100% phonetic. There are only a very few words that are pronounced slightly different from the way they are written.

You can use this book in combination with our Lao-English, English-Lao Dictionary for Non-Lao Speakers to expand your vocabulary and language usage.

We hope you enjoy this language course and are certain you will find it fun and worthwhile to communicate with the friendly Lao people in their own language.

Transliteration

Different Lao books and dictionaries use different transliteration systems. Many of them are oriented towards speakers of French and are not as helpful to English speakers. Every attempt was made to keep the transliteration in this book consistent, accurate and simple for English speakers. We use the standard international phonetic alphabet for tones and other sounds not normally represented in written English.

You will find that words are not always pronounced exactly as they are transliterated. In colloquial speech people speak fast, drop sounds and words, change some consonants (e.g. some people change "hoong-hian" to "loong-lian" - school), vowels, vowel length (e.g. "hiin" to "hin" - stone) and tones. Also, there are regional speech differences. We try to pick the pronunciation that is most widely and commonly used.

Five Tones vs Six Tones

Some linguists have identified six tones in the Lao language and others say there are five. According to the Lao high school textbooks published by the Ministry of Education of Laos, there are six tones in the northern dialect and five tones in the central and southern regions. The people in the north tend to speak more slowly and draw out words.

We use the five tone system in this book. It is the most commonly used and is the one promulgated by the Ministry of Education of Laos in their effort to standardize the Lao language.

Exceptions

Written Lao, especially as now standardized by the Lao government, is very phonetic. Nevertheless, some words are most commonly pronounced differently from the way they should be according to the rules of written Lao. This is especially true of multi-syllabic words in which tones and sounds can get dropped or changed in normal speech. When there is a difference between the way a word is written and the way it is spoken, we try to transliterate it according to the way it is most commonly spoken. For example, the word "post office" is transliterated as "bpai-sa-nii" instead of "bpai-sa-nii".

Changes in Tones

Even though Lao is tonal and each syllable has its own tone, Lao tends to change tones in many circumstances.

First, the tones of certain words can change according to where they are placed in a sentence. For example: people from the Vientiane area would change a middle consonant word from low tone to rising tone when it is placed at the end of a sentence or when it stands by itself (like when you hear it said on the audio). There is no change in tone when it is placed in the middle of a sentence.

e.g.   bpài is changed to bpǎi.
        kɔ̀i bɔɔ bpǎi. = I'm not going.
        kɔ̀i bɔɔ bpài dta-làat. = I'm not going to the market.
        dìi is changed to dǐi.
        sa-bàai-dǐi bɔɔ. = How are you?
        sa-bàai-dǐi. = I'm well.

Secondly, you may hear different tones for the same word in different regions. People in the north speak more slowly and tend do draw out words. For example the word "many" will sound more like a falling tone "lâai" rather than "lǎai" the rising tone. It also sounds longer.

Thirdly, people have different levels of tone or pitch when they speak. This oocurs in all languages but may be more noticeable in Lao. Keep this in mind when you hear individuals pronounce words in a non-standard way.

Finally, Lao has many ending particles. We do not explain the usage of all the particles in this book for beginners. Many ending particles are used to emphasize the needs and feelings of the speaker. They tend to change tones according to the nuances of the speaker's message.

You will hear different voices on our audio. The Lao speakers are from three regions of Laos. The two female voices are from Vientiane, one male speaker is from the north and one from the south.

Lao is a forgiving language when it comes to tones and pronunciation. Fortunately, since there is so much individual and regional variation, people are accustomed to hearing words pronounced in different ways. You will probably be understood in spite of imperfect tones and vowel length— assuming that you are not too far off and don't sound like you are saying something totally different!.

Table of Contents

Guide to Pronunciation

Consonants

b	as in baby	bìn - to fly
d	as in doll	dìi - good
f	as in fun	fái - fire
g	as in gold	gìn - eat
h	as in honey	hàa - five
j	as in jet	jĕt - seven
k	as in kiss	kón - person
l	as in love	líng - monkey
m	as in money	míi - to have
n	as in need	náa - rice field
ny	as in español	nyúng - mosquito
p	as in pretty	pán - thousand
s	as in sex	sii - four
t	as in tender	tŏng - bag
w	as in woman	wíi - fan
y	as in you	yàa - medicine
kw	as in queen	kwúan - smoke
gw	as in Guam	gwaa - more
ng	as in ringing	ngúu - snake
dt	as in stop	dtàa - eye
bp	as in spot	bpài - to go

The /dt/ sound lies between the /d/ and the /t/. Similarly, the /bp/ is between /b/ and /p/ (in linguistic terms, they are both unvoiced and unaspirated). Unlike English, /ng/ frequently occurs at the beginning of words in Lao.

Lao used to have the rolled "r" sound, but it has dropped out of common speech and been replaced by the "l" sound.

The new Lao writing system does not have consonant cluster sounds in either the initial or final position of a syllable. In this book final consonant sounds of a syllable are transliterated as follows:

k is used for ກ.

t is used for ດ.

p is used for ບ.

n is used for ນ.

ng is used for ງ.

m is used for ມ.

əi, əəi are used for ເꞮຍ.

aao is used for –າວ.

Vowels

Most Lao vowels have two versions, short and long. Short vowels are clipped and cut off at the end. Long ones are drawn out. This book shows short vowels with a single letter and long vowels with double letters ('a' for short; 'aa' for long).

The 'ʉ' has no comparable sound in English. Try saying 'u' while spreading your lips in as wide a smile as possible. If the sound you are making is similar to one you might have uttered after stepping on something disgusting, you are probably close!

Short & Long Vowels

a	like a in Alaska	mán - it
aa	like a in father	hàa - five
i	like i in tip	sǐp - ten
ii	like ee in see	sii - four
u	like oo in boot	yǔt - stop
uu	like u in ruler	sǔun - zero
ʉ	like u in ruler, but with a smile	nʉng - one
ʉʉ	like ʉ but longer	mʉ̀ʉ - hand
e	like e in pet	jět - seven
ee	like a in pale	péeng - song
ɛ	like a in cat	lɛ - and
ɛɛ	like a in sad	dɛ̀ɛng - red
ə	like er in teacher without the "r" sound	bəng - to look
əə	like ə but longer	bpə̀ət - open
o	like o in note	pǒm - hair
oo	like o in go	lôok - world
ɔ	like au in caught	gɔ́ - island
ɔɔ	like aw in law	nɔ́ɔn - to sleep

Complex Vowels

The following dipthongs are combinations of the above vowels.

ai	mai - new	aai	sáai - sand
ao	máo - drunk	aao	kǎao - white
ia	bìa - beer	iao	nǐao - sticky
ua	hǔa - head	uai	lúai - rich
ʉa	hʉ́a - boat	ʉai	mʉai - tired
ɔi	kɔ̀i - I, me	ɔɔi	nɔ́ɔi - little
ooi	dòoi - by	əəi	kə́əi - ever
ui	kui - flute	iu	hǐu - hungry
eo	leo - to fight	eeo	hěeo - cliff
ɛo	tɛ̌o - row	ɛɛo	lɛ̂ɛo - already

Short and Long Vowels Compared

Short Vowel			**Long Vowel**		
kǎo	(ເຂົາ)	horn	kǎao	(ຂາວ)	white
jàn	(ຈັນ)	moon	jàan	(ຈານ)	plate
nyáng	(ຍັງ)	yet	nyáang	(ຍາງ)	rubber oil
kún	(ຄຸນ)	gratitude	kúun	(ຄູນ)	to multiply
sǎi	(ໃສ)	clear	sǎai	(ສາຍ)	line
mài	(ໃໝ້)	burn	màai	(ໝ້າຍ)	widower
nái	(ໃນ)	in	náai	(ນາຍ)	master
háo	(ເຮົາ)	we	hǎao	(ຫາວ)	to yawn
jǎk	(ຈັກ)	machine	jàak	(ຈາກ)	from

Tone Marks

Because Lao is a tonal language, its pronunciation presents new challenges for English speakers. If the tone is wrong, you will not be easily understood even if everything else is correct. Lao uses five tones (some books say there are six). For example, to pronounce a rising tone your voice starts at a low pitch and goes up (much like asking a question in English). The phonetic transliteration in this book uses tone marks over the vowels to show the tone for each word. Note that the tone marks used for transliteration are different from those used in Lao script.

Tone Marks (Transliteration)

Tone	Tone Symbol	Example	
mid	None	maa	ໝາ
low	`	màa	ໝາ
falling	^	mâa	ມ້າ
high	´	máa	ມາ
rising	˘	mǎa	ໝາ

Some books use this mark ‿ for the low tone, e.g. maa.

Tones

Have a native speaker pronounce each tone using sample words in
the following pages. You listen to it, try to say it and see if you can
hear the tones correctly.

Samples of the five tones

Words with **mid** tone:

yuu	(ຢູ່)	to be, to live
bɔɔ	(ບໍ່)	no, not
sii	(ສີ່)	four
gai	(ໄກ່)	chicken
mii	(ໝີ່)	noodle

Words with **low** tone:

hàa	(ຫ້າ)	five
kào	(ເຂົ້າ)	rice, to enter
pàa	(ຜ້າ)	cloth
yàak	(ຢາກ)	to want
kài	(ໄຂ້)	sickness

Words with **falling** tone:

sâai	(ຊ້າຍ)	left
gâi	(ໃກ້)	near
nîi	(ນີ້)	this
sâo	(ເຊົ້າ)	morning
lîn	(ລີ້ນ)	tongue

Words with **high** tone:

kón	(ຄົນ)	person
láao	(ລາວ)	Lao
tái	(ໄທ)	Thai
hían	(ຮຽນ)	to study
náa	(ນາ)	rice field

Words with **rising** tone:

mǎa	(ໝາ)	dog
sǔung	(ສູງ)	tall
mǔu	(ໝູ)	pig
kǎao	(ຂາວ)	white
sǎam	(ສາມ)	three

Tones, Short-Long Vowels, Similar Consonants and Vowel Sounds

When you are not understood, often you are saying the tone wrong. However, the length of the vowel is also very important. Try to get the vowel length correct. This will help you to be understood better while you are still learning to master the tones.

Here are some examples of words with different tones and their meanings.

mâa	(ມ້າ)	horse
máa	(ມາ)	to come
mǎa	(ໝາ)	dog

mai	(ໃໝ່)	new
mài	(ໄໝ້)	to burn
mái	(ໄມ)	mile
mǎi	(ໄໝ)	silk

kaao	(ຂ່າວ)	news
káao	(ຄາວ)	fishy
kǎao	(ຂາວ)	white

kao	(ເຂົ່າ)	knee
kào	(ເຂົ້າ)	to enter, rice
kǎo	(ເຂົາ)	animal horn, he/she

sii	(ສີ່)	four
sǐi	(ສີ)	color

sùa	(ເສື້ອ)	shirt
sǔa	(ເສືອ)	tiger

hûu	(ຮູ້)	to know
húu	(ຮູ)	hole
hǔu	(ຫູ)	ear

Comparison of Similar Sounds

dìi	(ດີ)	good	dtìi	(ຕີ)	to hit
bài	(ໃບ)	leaf	bpài	(ໄປ)	to go
nǔu	(ໜູ)	mouse	ngúu	(ງູ)	snake
pět	(ເຜັດ)	spicy	bpět	(ເປັດ)	duck
kɯang	(ເຄື່ອງ)	machine	kɔ̀ng	(ເຄິ່ງ)	half
dào	(ເດົາ)	to guess	dtào	(ເຕົາ)	stove
pûɯn	(ພື້ນ)	floor	bpùɯn	(ປືນ)	gun

Lesson 1

greetings; yes-no questions; personal pronouns; cardinal and ordinal numbers; the Lao writing system; consonant classes; determining tones in written Lao; middle consonants; long vowels; tone marks

bŏt-tíi nʉng   ບົດທີ ໜຶ່ງ   Lesson 1

kám-sǎp   ຄຳສັບ   Vocabulary

kɔ̀i	ຂ້ອຍ	I, me
jâo/pûak-jâo	ເຈົ້າ /ພວກເຈົ້າ	you/you (plural)
sʉ̌ʉ	ຊື່	name
sa-bàai-dìi	ສະບາຍດີ	"Good day."
sa-bàai-dìi/sa-bàai-dìi-bɔɔ		"How are you?"[1]
ສະບາຍດີ /ສະບາຍດີບໍ?		
bpen-jang-dǎi	ເປັນຈັ່ງໃດ?	"How is it going?"
sa-bàai-dìi	ສະບາຍດີ	to be fine
yín-dii-tîi-dâi-pop-(gǎp)-jâo		Nice to meet you.
ຍິນດີທີ່ໄດ້ພົບ (ກັບ) ເຈົ້າ		
yín-dii-tîi-dâi-pop-jâo-kʉ̌ʉ-gan		Nice to meet you too.
ຍິນດີທີ່ໄດ້ພົບເຈົ້າຄືກັນ		
kɔ̌ɔ-tôot	ຂໍໂທດ	Excuse me.
bɔɔ-bpen-nyǎng	ບໍ່ເປັນຫຍັງ	It doesn't matter.[2]
kɔ̀ɔp-jài	ຂອບໃຈ	Thank you.
la/děe/dèe	ລະ (ແລ້ວ) /ເດ	"What about .....?"
bpûm	ປຶ້ມ	book
nǎng-sʉ̌ʉ-pím	ໜັງສືພິມ	newspaper
móong	ໂມງ	watch, clock
bpàak-gàa	ປາກກາ	pen
sɔ̌ɔ-dàm	ສໍດຳ	pencil
tǒng	ຖົງ	bag
pěɛn-tii	ແຜນທີ່	map
bpûm-kǐan	ປຶ້ມຂຽນ	notebook
nîi	ນີ້	this
nân	ນັ້ນ	that
pûun/pûn	ພຸ້ນ	that (further away)

mɛɛn/mɛn	ແມ່ນ	to be (something)[3]
nyǎng	ຫຍັງ	what
mɛɛn/mɛɛn-lέɛo	ແມ່ນ/ແມ່ນແລ້ວ	yes
bɔɔ	ບໍ່	no, not[4]
bɔɔ	ບໍ່	a question particle[4]
mɛɛn-bɔɔ	ແມ່ນບໍ່	..... right?
lǔu	ຫລື	or
gɔɔ	ກໍ່	also
kào-jai bɔɔ	ເຂົ້າໃຈບໍ່	Understand?
kào-jai	ເຂົ້າໃຈ	(I) understand.
bɔɔ kâo-jai	ບໍ່ເຂົ້າໃຈ	(I) don't understand.

1. sa-bàai-dìi can be used in greeting or leave-taking at any
   time of day or night.
2. bɔɔ-bpen-nyǎng has the following meanings: it doesn't matter;
   that's all right; not at all; it's nothing; never mind; don't
   mention it; forget it; you're welcome, etc.
3. You may hear this word pronounced either short or long.
4. bɔɔ (ບໍ່) is used to form a negative and used as a question particle
   placed at the end of sentences to form yes-no questions.
   e.g. dìi   = good
         bɔɔ dìi = not good
         dìi bɔɔ = Is it good?

Conversation 1

Jampa: sa-bàai-dìi.
ຈຳປາ :   ສະບາຍດີ .

                  Hello.

John: sa-bàai-dìi.
ຈອນ :   ສະບາຍດີ .

               Hello.

Jampa: kɔ̀i sɯ̄ɯ jàm-bpàa.   jâo sɯ̄ɯ nyǎng.
ຈຳປາ :   ຂ້ອຍ ຊື່   ຈຳປາ.   ເຈົ້າ ຊື່ ຫຍັງ .

                  My name is Supa. What's your name?

John: kɔ̀i sɯ̄ɯ jɔ̀ɔn.   yín-dìi tii dâi pop gǎp jâo.
ຈອນ :   ຂ້ອຍ ຊື່ ຈອນ.   ຍິນດີ   ທີ່ ໄດ້ ພົບ ກັບ ເຈົ້າ.

                  My name is John.   Nice to meet you.

Jampa: yín-dìi kɯ́ɯ-gan.
ຈຳປາ :   ຍິນດີ   ຄືກັນ .

               Nice to meet you, too.

Conversation 2

Kamsai: sa-bàai-dìi bɔɔ.
ຄຳໃສ :   ສະບາຍດີ   ບໍ?

                  How are you?

Ginny: sa-bàai dìi. lɛ̂ɛo jâo děe.
ຈິນນີ :   ສະບາຍດີ .   ແລ້ວ ເຈົ້າ ເດ?

                  I'm fine.   How about you?

Kamsai: kɔ̀i gɔɔ sa-bàai dìi. kɔ̀ɔp-jài.
ຄຳໃສ :   ຂ້ອຍ ກໍ່ ສະບາຍ ດີ .   ຂອບໃຈ.

                  I'm also fine.   Thank you.

bpà-nyòok   ปะโทยๆ   Sentences

1. A: nîi mɛɛn bpûm bɔɔ.
    ນີ້ ແມ່ນ ປື້ມ ບໍ?
    Is this a book?
    B: mɛɛn-lɛ́ɛo, nîi mɛɛn bpûm.
    ແມ່ນແລ້ວ ,ນີ້ ແມ່ນ ປື້ມ.
    Yes, this is a book.

2. A: nân mɛɛn bpûm-kǐan bɔɔ.
    ນັ້ນ ແມ່ນ ປື້ມຂຽນ ບໍ?
    Is that a notebook?
    B: bɔɔ, nan bɔɔ mɛɛn bpûm-kian.
    ບໍ, ນັ້ນ ບໍ່ ແມ່ນ ປື້ມຂຽນ.
    No, that is not a notebook.

3. A: nîi mɛɛn nyang.
    ນີ້ ແມ່ນ ຫຍັງ?
    What is this?
    B: nân mɛɛn tǒng.
    ນັ້ນ ແມ່ນ ຖົງ.
    That is a bag.

4. A: an-nîi mɛɛn móong lǔɨ bpàak-gaa.
    ອັນນີ້ ແມ່ນ ໂມງ ຫລື ປາກກາ?
    Is this a watch or a pen?
    B: an-nân bpàak-gaa.
    ອັນນັ້ນ ປາກກາ
    That is a pen.

5. A: kào-jài bɔɔ.
    ເຂົ້າໃຈ ບໍ?
    Do you understand?
    B: kào-jài.
    ເຂົ້າໃຈ
    Yes, (I understand).
    C: bɔɔ, bɔɔ kào-jài.
    ບໍ, ບໍ່ ເຂົ້າໃຈ
    No, (I don't understand).

6.   A: kɔ̌ɔ-tôot.

ຂໍໂທດ.

Excuse me.

B: bɔɔ bpèn-nyǎng.

ບໍ່   ເປັນຫຍັງ.

That's all right.

7.   A: kɔ̀ɔp-jài.

ຂອບໃຈ.

Thank you.

B: bɔɔ bpèn-nyǎng.

ບໍ່   ເປັນຫຍັງ.

You're welcome.

Notes: 1. A lot of Lao people greet each other with bpèn-jang-dǎi ເປັນຈັ່ງໃດ.
("How is it going?") instead of using sa-bàai-dìi bɔɔ.

2. The subject of a sentence is often omitted when understood from
the context.

e.g. A: jâo sa-bàai-dii bɔɔ. = sa-bàai-dii bɔ. (How are you?)

B: kɔ̀i sa-bàai-dii. =   sa-bàai-dii. (I'm fine.)

3. Lao has no direct "yes" or "no". We simply repeat the main verb or
adjective used in the question.

e.g. A: kào-jài bɔɔ. (Understand?)

B: kào-jài. (Understand.)

C: bɔɔ kào-jai. (Not understand.)

Be careful not to use "mɛɛn" for "yes" and "bɔɔ mɛɛn" for "no"
all the time. Use them primarily when the question is "mɛɛn bɔɔ".

jàm-núan ຈຳນວນ Numbers

0	sǔun	ສູນ
1	nùng	ໜຶ່ງ, ນຶ່ງ
2	sɔ̌ɔng	ສອງ
3	sǎam	ສາມ
4	sii	ສີ່
5	hàa	ຫ້າ
6	hǒk	ຫົກ
7	jět	ເຈັດ
8	bpὲɛt	ແປດ
9	gâo	ເກົ້າ
10	sǐp	ສິບ
11	sǐp-ět	ສິບເອັດ
12	sǐp-sɔ̌ɔng	ສິບສອງ
13	sǐp-sǎam	ສິບສາມ
20	sáao	ຊາວ
21	sáao-èt	ຊາວເອັດ
22	sáao-sɔ̌ɔng	ຊາວສອງ
30	sǎam-sǐp	ສາມສິບ
31	sǎam-sǐp-ět	ສາມສິບເອັດ
32	sǎam-sǐp-sɔ̌ɔng	ສາມສິບສອງ
40	sii-sìp	ສີ່ສິບ
50	hàa-sǐp	ຫ້າສິບ
60	hǒk-sǐp	ຫົກສິບ
70	jět-sǐp	ເຈັດສິບ
80	bpὲɛt-sǐp	ແປດສິບ
90	gâo-sǐp	ເກົ້າສິບ
100	(nùng) hɔ̂ɔi	(ໜຶ່ງ) ຮ້ອຍ*
200	sɔ̌ɔng-hɔ̂ɔi	ສອງຮ້ອຍ

300	săam-hɔ̂ɔi	ສາມຮ້ອຍ
1,000	(nùng) pán	(ໜຶ່ງ) ພັນ
2,000	sɔ̌ɔng-pán	ສອງພັນ
3,000	săam-pán	ສາມພັນ
10,000	(nùng) mùùn/sĭp-pán	(ໜຶ່ງ) ໝື່ນ/ສິບພັນ
100,000	(nùng) sɛ̌ɛn/hɔ̂ɔi-pán	(ໜຶ່ງ) ແສນ/ຮ້ອຍພັນ
1,000,000	(nùng) lâan	(ໜຶ່ງ) ລ້ານ
10,000,000	sĭp lâan	ສິບລ້ານ
100,000,000	(nùng) hɔ̂ɔi lâan	(ໜຶ່ງ) ຮ້ອຍລ້ານ
1,000,000,000	(nùng) pán lâan/dtùù	(ໜຶ່ງ) ພັນລ້ານ/ຕື້
10,000,000,000	(nùng) mùùn lâan	(ໜຶ່ງ) ໝື່ນລ້ານ
100,000,000,000	(nùng) sɛ̌ɛn lâan	(ໜຶ່ງ) ແສນລ້ານ
1,000,000,000,000	(nùng) lâan lâan/gòot	(ໜຶ່ງ) ລ້ານລ້ານ/ໂກດ

1.3	nung jŭt săam	ໜຶ່ງຈຸດສາມ
2 3/5	sɔ̌ɔng gǎp săam suan hàa	ສອງກັບສາມສ່ວນຫ້າ
7^2	jĕt gàm-láng sɔ̌ɔng	ເຈັດກຳລັງສອງ

* "hɔ̂ɔi" is sometimes pronounced "lɔ̂ɔi".

Notes: For ordinal numbers, add tîi (ທີ) in front of cardinal numbers.

e.g.   tîi nung (ທີໜຶ່ງ) = the first
       tîi sɔ̌ɔng (ທີສອງ) = the second
       tîi săam (ທີສາມ) = the third
       tîi sĭp (ທີສິບ) = the tenth

Test 1

Match the English words with the Lao words.

_____	1. watch	a. yăng	ຫຍັງ
_____	2. book	b. bpàak-gàa	ປາກກາ
_____	3. pen	c. nîi	ນີ້
_____	4. this	d. kɔ̀i	ຂ້ອຍ
_____	5. I	e. móong	ໂມງ
_____	6. also	f. nân	ນັ້ນ
_____	7. map	g. kɔ̀i	ຂ້ອຍ
_____	8. name	h. sɰɰ	ຊື່
_____	9. what	i. tŏng	ຖົງ
_____	10. bag	j. bpɰ̂m	ປຶ້ມ
		k. pɛ̆ɛn-tii	ແຜນທີ່
		l. gɔɔ	ກໍ່

Translate the following into English.

1. jâo sa-bàai dìi bɔɔ. ເຈົ້າ ສະບາຍດີ ບໍ່?

    _____

2. kâo-jài bɔɔ. ເຂົ້າໃຈບໍ່?

    _____

3. nîi mɛɛn năng-sɰɰ-pím mɛɛn bɔɔ. ນີ້ ແມ່ນ ຫນັງສືພິມ ແມ່ນ ບໍ່?

    _____

4. jâo sɰɰ nyăng. ເຈົ້າ ຊື່ ຫຍັງ?

    _____

5. an-nîi mɛɛn pɛ̆ɛn-tii lɰɰ sɔ̆ɔ-dam. ອັນນີ້ ແມ່ນ ແຜນທີ່ ຫລື ສໍດຳ?

    _____

The Lao Writing System

Lao uses an alphabet of 26 consonants, 28 vowels, four tone marks (only two commonly used) and various other symbols for punctuation, numbers, etc. Although there are irregular pronunciations, Lao is generally phonetic. It is pronounced the way it is written. It is even more phonetic than Thai, its relative.

Learning to read and write Lao from the beginning has many advantages. Due to the fact that it is phonetic, you will be reinforcing your listening and speaking skills while learning to read and write. In fact, most people find that their pronunciation is more accurate when reading Lao script. Unlike many transliteration systems, it incorporates all the elements of pronunciation— including tones and vowel length.

The longer you rely on transliteration, the more time you waste reinforcing a writing system that will be virtually useless in Laos. Furthermore, transliteration is a confusing hodgepodge with almost as many systems as there are books about Laos. Put a little extra effort into learning the alphabet now! Then you can use Lao script while studying conversation, reinforcing reading and writing skills that will be invaluable to you in Laos.

Consonant Classes

Lao consonants are divided into three classes— high, middle and low. Since it is one of the critical factors in determining a syllable's tone, you must know the consonant class in order to correctly pronounce what you have read.

The names (high, middle and low) of the consonant classes are completely arbitrary. For example, a low consonant may generate a high tone and a high consonant can generate a low tone, etc.

What Determines the Tone

1.   Consonant class: whether the initial consonant is high, middle or low.

2.   Vowel length: whether short or long.

3.   Tone Mark: whether or not there is a tone mark placed above the initial consonant of a syllable. (If the consonant has a superscript vowel, the tone mark is placed above that vowel.)

4.   Final consonant: whether sonorant final or stop final.

Middle Consonants

ອັກສອນກາງ (ăk-sɔ̌ɔn-gàang)

There are eight "middle" consonants in Lao as follows:

Consonant		Consonant Name	Sound
ກ	ກ ໄກ່	gɔ̀ɔ gai - chicken	/g/
ຈ	ຈ ຈອກ	jɔ̀ɔ jɔ̀ɔk - cup, glass	/j/
ດ	ດ ເດັກ	dɔ̀ɔ dĕk - child	/d/
ຕ	ຕ ຕາ	dtɔ̀ɔ dtaa - eye	/dt/
ບ	ບ ແບ້	bɔ̀ɔ bɛ̂ɛ - goat	/b/
ປ	ປ ປາ	bpɔ̀ɔ bpàa - fish	/bp/
ຢ	ຢ ຢາ	yɔ̀ɔ yàa - medicine	/y/
ອ	ອ ໂອ	ɔ̀ɔ òo - bowl	/silent/

Practice Writing the Middle Consonants

All the middle consonants are written with one stroke starting near the **❶**. Notice that you always start with the small circle where there is one.

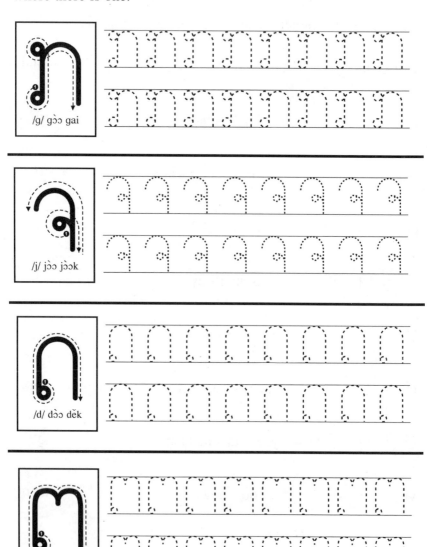

/g/ gɔ̀ɔ gai

/j/ jɔɔ jɔ̀ɔk

/d/ dɔɔ dĕk

/dt/ dtɔɔ dtàa

/b/ bɔɔ bɛ̂ɛ

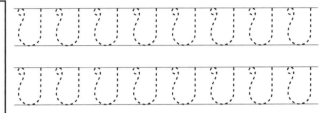

/bp/ bpɔɔ bpàa

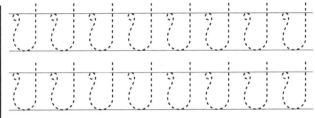

/y/ yɔɔ yàa

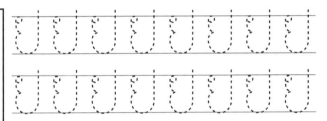

/ɔ/ ɔɔ ɔ̀ɔ

Vowels ສະຫລະ (sà-lǎ)

Lao has two kinds of vowels: short and long. In this lesson we will learn the following **long vowels**. Every Lao syllable starts with a consonant (even if the consonant is a silent ອ /-/). Although the consonant sound comes first, the vowel may be written before, above, below, after or around the consonant depending on the vowel. In the examples below, the dash represents the place where the consonant should be written.

Vowel	Vowel Name	Sound
– า	sà-lǎ àa	/aa/
–ີ	sà-lǎ ìi	/ii/
–ູ	sà-lǎ ùu	/uu/
ເ–	sà-lǎ èe	/ee/
ໂ–	sà-lǎ òo	/oo/
ໄ–	sà-lǎ ǎi	/ai/
ເ–ົາ	sà-lǎ ào	/ao/

Practice Writing the Following Vowels

Use ອ /-/ as the consonant when practicing the following vowels. Always start with the small circle where there is one.

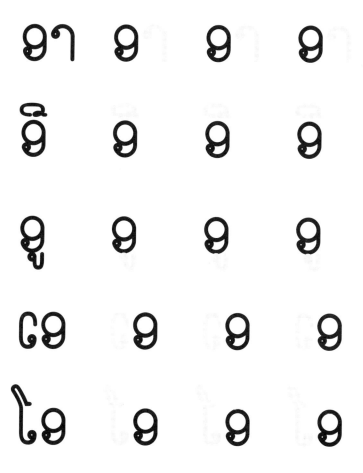

ไอ ไอ ไอ ไอ

เอ๊า เอา เอา เอา

Read The Following Aloud

1. ກາ   ກຶ   ກຸ   ເກາ   ໄກ   ໃກ   ເກົາ
2. ຈາ   ຈຶ   ຈຸ   ເຈາ   ໄຈ   ໃຈ   ເຈົາ
3. ຄາ   ຄຶ   ຄຸ   ເຄາ   ໄຄ   ໃຄ   ເຄົາ
4. ຕາ   ຕຶ   ຕຸ   ເຕາ   ໄຕ   ໃຕ   ເຕົາ
5. ບາ   ບຶ   ບຸ   ເບາ   ໄບ   ໃບ   ເບົາ
6. ປາ   ປຶ   ປຸ   ເປາ   ໄປ   ໃປ   ເປົາ
7. ອາ   ອຶ   ອຸ   ເອາ   ໄອ   ໃອ   ເອົາ

Tone Marks (Lao Script)

Lao has four tone marks. (The first two are more commonly used.) When a tone mark is used, it is always placed above the initial consonant of the syllable. If the consonant has a superscript vowel, the tone mark is placed above that vowel.

Tone Mark	Name
່ —	mâi èek (ໄມ້ເອກ)
້ —	mâi tóo (ໄມ້ໂທ)
໊ —	mâi dtìi (ໄມ້ຕີ)
໋ —	mâi jăt-dta-wáa (ໄມ້ຈັດຕະວາ)

Tone Marks With Middle Consonants

   With middle consonant syllables, all five tones are possible
and all four tone marks can be used. The high and rising tones are
not seen very often.

Tone Mark	Tone Name	Tone	Examples
่ —	sĭang săa-mán	mid	กา (gaa)
None	sĭang èek	low	ก่า (gàa)
้ —	sĭang too	falling	ก้า (gâa)
๊ —	sĭang dtìi	high	ก๊า (gáa)
๋ + —	sĭang jăt-dta-wáa	rising	ก๋า (găa)

Read The Following Aloud

1. ก่า   กา   ก้า

2. กิ่   กิ   กิ้

3. งุ่   งุ   งุ้

4. เก่   เก   เก้

5. ไก่   ไก   ไก้

6.　ໄກ່　ໄກ　ໄກ້

7.　ເກົາ　ເກົາ　ເກົາ

8.　ຈີ່　ຈີ　ຈີ້

9.　ຈຸ່　ຈຸ　ຈຸ້

10.　ເຈົາ　ເຈົາ　ເຈົາ

11.　ໄຈ່　ໄຈ　ໄຈ້

12.　ໄຈ່　ໄຈ　ໄຈ້

13.　ເຈົາ　ເຈົາ　ເຈົາ

14.　ຄຸ່　ຄຸ　ຄຸ້

15.　ເຄົາ　ເຄົາ　ເຄົາ

16.　ໄຄ່　ໄຄ　ໄຄ້

17.　ໄຄ່　ໄຄ　ໄຄ້

18.　ເຄົາ　ເຄົາ　ເຄົາ

19.　ເທົ່າ　ເທົາ　ເທົ້າ

20.　ໄທ່　ໄທ　ໄທ້

21.　ໄທ່　ໄທ　ໄທ້

22.　ເທົາ　ເທົາ　ເທົາ

23.　ໄບ່　ໄບ　ໄບ້

24.　ໄບ່　ໄບ　ໄບ້

25.　ໄບ່　ໄບ　ໄບ້

26.　ເບົາ　ເບົາ　ເບົາ

Writing Exercise 1

Transcribe the following into Lao script.

1. dàa _____   11. jài _____

2. gǒo _____   12. dtao _____

3. bâi _____   13. òo _____

4. dtuu _____   14. bpài _____

5. ào _____   15. gûu _____

6. bpǒo_____   16. bǒo _____

7. gao _____   17. jâa _____

8. jîi _____   18. dào _____

9. âi _____   19. gii _____

10. bêe _____   20. âa _____

Lesson 2

'bpèn', 'yuu' (to be); more vowels; live and dead
syllables; tone rules for middle consonants

bŏt-tii sɔ̌ɔng   ບົດທິ ສອງ   Lesson 2

kám-săp   ຄຳສັບ   Vocabulary

tóo-la-săp ໂທລະສັບ		telephone
tóo-la-tat ໂທລະທັດ		television
wɛn-dtaa ແຫວ່ນຕາ		eye-glasses
ngə́n ເງິນ		money
wat-ja-náa-nu-gòm		dictionary
ວັດຈະນານຸກົມ		
hûup/hûup-pâap ຮູບ /ຮູບພາບ		picture
jîa ເຈັ້ຍ		paper
dto ໂຕະ		table
gâo-îi ເກົ້າອີ້		chair
hɔ̀ng ຫ້ອງ		room
hɔ̀ng-nɔ́ɔn ຫ້ອງນອນ		bedroom
hɔ̀ng-nâm ຫ້ອງນ້ຳ		bathroom
hɯ́an ເຮືອນ		house
bpèn ເປັນ		to be something
yuu ຢູ່		to be somewhere (live, stay)
ào ເອົາ		to get, take, want
nái ໃນ		in
tə́ng ເທິງ		on
dtâi/lum ໃຕ້/ລຸ່ມ		under
la-waang/waang-gàang		between
ລະຫວ່າງ/ຫວ່າງກາງ		
găp ກັບ		and, with
bɔɔ dâi ບໍ່ໄດ້		not
mɯ́ang ເມືອງ		town, city

kón	ຄົນ	person
kón láao	ຄົນລາວ	Laotian
kón tái	ຄົນໄທ	Thai
kón jìin	ຄົນຈີນ	Chinese
kón nyii-bpun	ຄົນຍີ່ປຸ່ນ	Japanese
kón àa-mée-li-gàa	ຄົນອາເມລິກາ	American[1]
kón fa-lang	ຄົນຝຣັ່ງ	Frenchman[1]
kón gào-lǐi	ຄົນເກົາຫລີ	Korean
kón àng-gǐt	ຄົນອັງກິດ	Englishman
kón-kǎai-kʉang	ຄົນຂາຍເຄື່ອງ	vendor
bpa-têet	ປະເທດ	country
bpa-têet láao/mʉang-láao		Laos
ປະເທດລາວ / ເມືອງລາວ		
bpa-têet tái/mʉang-tái		Thailand
ປະເທດໄທ / ເມືອງໄທ		
bpa-têet jìin	ປະເທດຈີນ	China
bpa-têet yii-bpun	ປະເທດຍີ່ປຸ່ນ	Japan
bpa-têet àa-mée-li-gàa		America
ປະເທດອາເມລິກາ		
bpa-têet àng-gǐt	ປະເທດອັງກິດ	England
páa-sǎa	ພາສາ	language
páa-sǎa láao	ພາສາລາວ	Lao language
páa-sǎa àng-gǐt	ພາສາອັງກິດ	English language
tii	ທີ່	at
yuu-nìi	ຢູ່ນີ້	(over) here
yuu-hàn	ຢູ່ຫັ້ນ	(over) there
yuu-pûn	ຢູ່ພຸ້ນ	(over) there (further)
yuu-sǎi	ຢູ່ໃສ	where
táang	ທາງ	way
sâai	ຊ້າຍ	left

kwŭa/kwăa	ຂວາ	right
àn-nîi	ອັນນີ້	this one
àn-nân	ອັນນັ້ນ	that one
an-pûn	ອັນພຸ້ນ	that one (further away)
an-dăi	ອັນໃດ	which one
tao-dăi	ເທົ່າໃດ	how much[2]
jăk	ຈັກ	how many[2]
gìip	ກີບ	kip
dɔ̀n/dɔ̀n-lâa	ດອນ/ ດອນລາ	dollar
yèn	ເຢັນ	yen
tɯ̀ɯk	ຖຶກ	cheap
péɛng	ແພງ	expensive
nyâak	ຍາກ	difficult
ngaai	ງ່າຍ	easy
lăai	ຫລາຍ	very, many
háo/pûak háo	ເຮົາ/ ພວກເຮົາ	we, us
láao/pən	ລາວ/ ເພິ່ນ	he, she, him, her[3]
kăo-jâo/pûak-kăo	ເຂົາເຈົ້າ/ ພວກເຂົາ	they, them
mán	ມັນ	it

1. You may see different spellings of these words.

2. You use tâo-dăi (ເທົ່າໃດ) , which means "how much", without a classifier when asking about the quantity of uncountable nouns. But jăk (ຈັກ) which means "how many" must be followed by a classifier.

   e.g. 1. an-nîi tao-dăi. = How much is this one?

   2. an-nîi jăk gìip. = How many kip is this one?

   tâo-dăi (ເທົ່າໃດ) is often pronounced tɔɔ-dăi (ທໍໃດ) .

3. láao (he, she) is written the same as the word láao (Laotian). pən is used to refer to someone who is older or who the speaker has respect for.

Conversation 1

Bua: kɔ̀i bpèn kón láao. jâo bpèn kón nyǎng.

ບົວ: ຂ້ອຍ ເປັນ ຄົນ ລາວ. ເຈົ້າ ເປັນ ຄົນ ຫຍັງ?

I'm Lao. What nationality are you?

Tony: kɔ̀i bpèn kón àa-mée-li-gàn.

ໂທນີ່:   ຂ້ອຍ ເປັນ ຄົນ   ອາເມລິກັນ.

I'm American.

Bua: jâo yuu sǎi.

ບົວ: ເຈົ້າ ຢູ່ ໃສ?

Where do you live?

Tony: kɔ̀i yuu sɛɛn-di-ee-gôo.

ໂທນີ່:   ຂ້ອຍ ຢູ່   ແຊນດິເອໂກ້.

I live in San Diego.

jâo děe.

ເຈົ້າ ເດ?

And you?

Bua: kɔ̀i yuu wíang-jàn.

ບົວ: ຂ້ອຍ ຢູ່   ວຽງຈັນ.

I live in Vianetiane.

Conversation 2

Jim: an-nîi tao-dǎi.

จิມ: ອັນນີ້   ເທົ່າໃດ?

>   How much is this one?

Konkǎai: sii-sǐp pán gìip.

ຄົນຂາຍ: ສີ່ສິບ   ພັນ   ກີບ.

>   Forty thousand kip.

Jim: ôo, pέεng pôot.

จิມ: ໂອ, ແພງ   ໂພດ.

>   Oh, that's too expensive.

>   àn-nân dêe jǎk gìip.

>   ອັນນັ້ນ   ເດ   ຈັກ ກີບ?

>   How much is that one?

Konkǎai: sǎam-sǐp pán gìip.

ຄົນຂາຍ: ສາມສິບ   ພັນ   ກີບ.

>   Thirty thousand kip.

Jim: bɔɔ pέεng bpàan-dǎi. kɔ̀i ào àn-nîi lǎ.*

จิມ: ບໍ່   ແພງ   ປານໃດ.   ຂ້ອຍ ເອົາ ອັນນີ້ ລະ.

>   That's not so expensive. I take this one.

Konkǎai: kɔ̀ɔp-jài lǎai-lǎai.

ຄົນຂາຍ: ຂອບໃຈ   ຫລາຍໆ.

>   Thank you very much.

Jim: bɔɔ bpèn nyǎng.

จิມ: ບໍ່   ເປັນ   ຫຍັງ.

>   You're welcome.

*An ending particle

bpà-nyòok   ປະໂທຍກ   Sentences

1. A: tóo-la-sǎp yuu sǎi.
       ໂທລະສັບ   ຢູ່ ໃສ?
       Where is the phone?

    B: tóo-la-sǎp yuu táng dto.
       ໂທລະສັບ   ຢູ່ ເທິງ ໂຕະ.
       The phone is on the table.

    C: jâo yuu sǎi.
       ເຈົ້າ ຢູ່ ໃສ?
       Where are you?

    D: kòi yuu hứan.
       ຂ້ອຍ ຢູ່ ເຮືອນ.
       I'm at home.

    E: láao yuu sǎi.
       ລາວ ຢູ່ ໃສ?
       Where is he?

    F: láao yuu nìi.
       ລາວ ຢູ່ ໜີ້.
       He is here.

    G: hòng-nâm yuu sǎi.
       ຫ້ອງນ້ຳ   ຢູ່ ໃສ?
       Where is the bathroom?

    H: hòng-nâm yuu táang sâai.
       ຫ້ອງນ້ຳ   ຢູ່ ທາງ ຊ້າຍ.
       The bathroom is on the left.

2. A: jâo bpèn kón nyǎng.
       ເຈົ້າ ເປັນ ຄົນ ຫຍັງ?
       What nationality are you?

    B: kòi bpèn kón àa-mée-li-gàa.
       ຂ້ອຍ ເປັນ ຄົນ ອາເມລິກາ.
       I am American.

    C: pǝn bpèn kón nyǎng.
       ເພິ່ນ ເປັນ ຄົນ ຫຍັງ?
       What nationality is he?

D: pən bpèn kón láao.
ເພິ່ນ ເປັນ ຄົນ ລາວ.
He is Lao.

E: taan táa-náa-gǎ bpèn kón nyǎng.
ທ່ານ ທານາກະ ເປັນ ຄົນ ຫຍັງ?
What nationality is Mrs. Tanaka?

F: pən bpèn kón nyii-bpun.
ເພິ່ນ ເປັນ ຄົນ ຍີ່ປຸ່ນ.
She is Japanese.

3. A: an-nîi tao-dǎi.
ອັນ ນີ້ ເທົ່າໃດ?
How much is this one?

B: an-nîi hàa-sǐp-pán gìip.
ອັນນີ້ ຫ້າສິບພັນ ກີບ.
This one is 50,0000 kip.

C: an-nân tao-dǎi.
ອັນ ນັ້ນ ເທົ່າໃດ?
How much is that one?

D: 2,000 yeen.
2,000 ເຢັນ
2,000 yen.

E: àn-nân tao-dǎi.
ອັນນັ້ນ ເທົ່າໃດ?
How much is that?

F: àn-nîi 6 dɔ̀n (lâa).
ອັນນີ້ 6 ດອນ(ລ່າ)
This is 6 dollars.

4. A: tóo-la-sǎp yuu tóng dto mɛɛn bɔɔ.
ໂທລະສັບ ຢູ່ ເທິງ ໂຕະ ແມ່ນ ບໍ?
Is the phone on the table?

B: mɛɛn-léɛo, tóo-la-sǎp yuu tóng dtó.
ແມ່ນແລ້ວ, ໂທລະສັບ ຢູ່ ເທິງ ໂຕະ.
Yes, the phone is on the table.

C: bɔɔ, tóo-la-sǎp bɔɔ dǎi yuu tóng dto.
ບໍ່, ໂທລະສັບ ບໍ່ ໄດ້ ຢູ່ ເທິງ ໂຕະ.
No, the phone is not on the table.

5. A: kǎo-jâo bpèn kón nyii-bpun lǔu kón gào-lǐi.
       ເຂົາເຈົ້າ ເປັນ ຄົນ ຍີ່ປຸ່ນ ຫລື ຄົນ ເກົາຫລີ.
       Are they Japanese or Korean?

    B: kǎo-jâo bpèn kón gào-lǐi.
       ເຂົາເຈົ້າ ເປັນ ຄົນ ເກົາຫລີ?
       They are Korean.

6. A: jâo bpèn kón laao mɛɛn bɔɔ.
       ເຈົ້າ ເປັນ ຄົນ ລາວ ແມ່ນ ບໍ່?
       Are you Lao?

    B: mɛɛn, kɔi bpèn kón láao.
       ແມ່ນ, ຂ້ອຍ ເປັນ ຄົນ ລາວ.
       Yes, I'm Lao.

    C: bɔɔ mɛɛn, kɔi bpèn kón tai.
       ບໍ່ ແມ່ນ, ຂ້ອຍ ເປັນ ຄົນ ໄທ.
       No, I'm Thai.

7. A: páa-sǎa láao nyâak bɔɔ.
       ພາສາ ລາວ ຍາກ ບໍ່?
       Is Lao difficult?

    B: nyâak.
       ຍາກ
       Yes. (Difficult)

    C: bɔɔ yâak.
       ບໍ່ ຍາກ.
       No. (Not difficult)

8. A: páa-sǎa láao ngaai.
       ພາສາ ລາວ ງ່າຍ.
       Lao is easy.

    B: páa-sǎa láao bɔɔ ngaai.
       ພາສາ ລາວ ບໍ່ ງ່າຍ.
       Lao is not easy.

    C: páa-sǎa àng-gǐt yâak.
       ພາສາ ອັງກິດ ຍາກ.
       English is difficult.

    D: páa-sǎa àng-gǐt bɔɔ yâak.
       ພາສາ ອັງກິດ ບໍ່ ຍາກ.
       English is not difficult.

9. A: àn-n̂ii pɛ́ɛng.

ອັນ ນີ້ ແພງ.

This one is expensive.

    B: àn-n̂ii bɔɔ pɛ́ɛng.

—   ອັນ ນີ້ ບໍ່ ແພງ.

This one is not expensive.

10.   bpûm yuu waang-gàang dto găp gâo-îi.

ປຶ້ມ ຢູ່ ທ່າງກາງ ໂຕະ ກັບ ຕັ່ງອີ້.

The book is between the table and the chair.

Notes: 1. 'taan' means "you", and it is placed in front of people's first
names or last names to address them in a polite way.

      2. 'bɔɔ dâi' is a negative form like 'not' in English, and is
used with verbs. It also means 'cannot' (see lesson 3) and
'did not' (see lesson 7).
e.g. bpûm <u>bɔɔ dâi</u> yuu tə́ng dto. = bpûm <u>bɔɔ</u> yuu təng dto.
(The book is not on the table.)

      3. bɔɔ mɛɛn is a negative form like 'no' or 'not', and is
used with nouns.
e.g. kɔ̀i <u>bɔɔ mɛɛn</u> kón nyii-bpun. (I'm not Japanese.)

      4. There is no exact 'yes' or 'no' in Lao. To answer 'yes', simply
repeat the verb or the adjective used in the question. To
answer 'no', put bɔɔ before the appropriate word
(see sentence number 7).

Test 2

Match the English words with the Lao words.

_____ 1. chair   a. tóo-la-săp ໂຕະລະສັບ

_____ 2. table   b. dtâi ໃຕ້

_____ 3. money   c. sɔ̌ɔ-dàm ສຳດຳ

_____ 4. Lao people   d. pən ເພິ່ນ

_____ 5. Japanese   e. kón ang-gĭt ຄົນອັງກິດ

_____ 6. Englishman   f. pέɛng ແພງ

_____ 7. in   g. tə́ng ເທິງ

_____ 8. on   h. nyâak ຍາກ

_____ 9. under   i. mʉang ເມືອງ

_____ 10. telephone   j. hɔ̀ng-nɔ́ɔn ຫ້ອງນອນ

_____ 11. bedroom   k. dto ໂຕະ

_____ 12. television   l. kón láao ຄົນລາວ

_____ 13. he/she   m. gâo-îi ເກົ້າອີ້

_____ 14. expensive   n. ngə́n ເງິນ

_____ 15. difficult   o. kón yii-bpun ຄົນຍີ່ປຸ່ນ

                              p. nái ໃນ

                              q. tóo-la-tat ໂຕະລະທັດ

                              r. tʉ̀ʉk ຖຶກ

Translate the following into English.

1. tóo-la-sǎp yuu táng gâo-îi.
    ໂທລະສັບ   ຢູ່   ເທິງ ເກົ້າອີ້.

_____

2. láao bpèn kón jìin, bɔɔ mɛɛn kón yîi-bpun.
    ລາວ   ເປັນ ຄົນ ຈີນ, ບໍ່ ແມ່ນ ຄົນ ຍີ່ປຸ່ນ.

_____

3. an-nîi tao-dǎi.
    ອັນ ນີ້ ເທົ່າໃດ?

_____

4. hɔ̀ng-nâm yuu sǎi.
    ຫ້ອງນ້ຳ   ຢູ່ ໃສ?

_____

5. páa-sǎa àng-gǐt nyâak lǎai.
    ພາສາ   ອັງກິດ   ຍາກ   ຫລາຍ.

_____

More Vowels

The vowels below include those from lesson one plus five more. Each has a corresponding short vowel form. The difference between a short and long vowel is an important one— it can change a word's meaning by itself. Also, the tone rules for short and long vowels are different.

<u>Short Vowel</u>		<u>Long Vowel</u>	
1. $-\breve{\circ}$	/ăɟ	$-ๅ$	/àa/
2. $\overset{\circ}{-}$	/ĭ/	$\overset{๏}{-}$	/ìi/
3. $\overset{\circ}{-}$	/ŭ/	$\overset{๏}{-}$	/ùu/
4. $\underset{ุ}{-}$	/ŭ/	$\underset{ู}{-}$	/ùu/
5. $\complement-\breve{\circ}$	/ĕ/	$\complement-$	/èe/
6. $\complement\complement-\breve{\circ}$	/ɛ̆/	$\complement\complement-$	/ɛ̀ɛ/
7. $\mathfrak{l}-\breve{\circ}$	/ŏ/	$\mathfrak{l}-$	/òo/
8. $\complement-ๅ\breve{\circ}$	/ɔ̆/	$\overset{\circ}{-}$	/ɔ̀ɔ/

9. ເ◌̆ /ə̆/   ເ◌̂ /əə/

10. ◌ົວະ /ŭa/   ◌ົວ /ùa/

11. ເ◌ັຍ /ĭa/   ເ◌ຍ /ìa/

12. ເ◌̆ອ /ŭa/   ເ◌̂ອ /ùa/

Practice Writing the Following Vowels

Use ອ /-/ as the consonant when practicing the following vowels.

 ອ ອ ອ

 ອ ອ ອ

 ອ ອ ອ

ໍ່ຶ   ຶ   ຶ   ຶ

ເຶ່ອ   ຶ   ຶ

ເຶ້ອ   ຶ   ຶ

ເຶ໋ຍ   ຶ   ຶ

ເຶຍ   ຶ   ຶ

ເຶ່ອ   ຶ   ຶ

ເຶ້ອ   ຶ   ຶ

ອີວະ   ອີວະ   ອີວະ

ອີວ   ອີວ   ອີວ   ອີວ

Read The Following Aloud

1. ກະ   ກາ   ຈະ   ຈາ
2. ກິ   ກີ   ດິ   ດີ
3. ກຶ   ກື   ຕຶ   ຕື
4. ກຸ   ກູ   ບຸ   ບູ
5. ເກະ   ເກ   ເປະ   ເປ
6. ແກະ   ແກ   ແອະ   ແອ
7. ໂກະ   ໂກ   ໂຈະ   ໂຈ
8. ເກາະ   ກຳ   ເຄາະ   ຄຳ
9. ເກິ   ເກີ   ເຊື   ເຊື
10. ເກັຍ   ເກຍ   ເບັຍ   ເບຍ
11. ເກຶອະ   ເກືອ   ເປຶອະ   ເປືອ
12. ກິວະ   ກິວ   ຕົວະ   ຕົວ

Live and Dead Syllables
(ຄຳເປັນ–ຄຳຕາຍ)

Every Lao syllable is pronounced with one of the five tones, whether it has a tone mark or not. When there is no tone mark, tone rules apply. In that case, the tone is determined by consonant class and whether the syllable is live or dead.

A syllable that ends with a short vowel or a stop final consonant is called a dead syllable.

A syllable that ends with a long vowel or a sonorant final consonant is called a live syllable.

For now, just consider the short and long vowels, since we haven't introduced final consonants yet.

Tone Rules for Middle Consonants

In the absence of a tone mark, the tone rules for middle consonants are as follows:

Middle Consonant with Live Syllable = Low Tone

Middle Consonant with Dead Syllable = Rising Tone

Examples:

Middle Consonant + Long Vowel = Low Tone

	Sound Produced	Meaning
ก + –า–	= กา (gàa)	crow
บ + ไ–	= ไบ (bpài)	to go
อ + เ–า	= เอา (ào)	to take

Reading Exercise: <u>Read the Following Words and Practice Writing Them in Lao.</u>

1.	ດີ	good	2.	ໃຈ	heart
3.	ຕາ	eye	4.	ເກົາ	to scratch
5.	ອາ	uncle	6.	ເຕົາ	stove
7.	ບົວ	lotus	8.	ແຈ	corner
9.	ປີ	year	10.	ປູ	crab
11.	ໄອ	to cough	12.	ເບຍ	beer
13.	ຈໍ	screen	14.	ໂຕ	body

Middle Consonant + Short Vowel = Rising Tone

	Sound Produced	Meaning
ກ + ເ−າະ	= ເກາະ (gɔ̌)	island
ຈ + −ະ	= ຈະ (jǎ)	will
ຕ + ເ−ະ	= ເຕະ (dtě)	to kick

Reading Exercise: <u>Read the Following Words and Practice Writing Them in Lao.</u>

1. ຕໍ   to criticize   2. ຈຸ   capacity

3. ບຸ   to put in a lining   4. ເຈາະ   to drill

5. ປະ   to patch (cloth)   6. ເບາະ   cushion

7. ເກະກະ   disorderly

Writing Exercise 2

Transcribe the following into Lao script.

1. bàa _____   11. gʉa _____

2. gɛ̌ _____   12. dtɔ̀ɔ _____

3. bʉ̀a _____   13. ʉ̀ʉ _____

4. dtʉ̌ _____   14. bpǎ _____

5. bɔ̀ɔ _____   15. gʉ̌ _____

6. jèe _____   16. dtɔ̌ _____

7. gǐ _____   17. ə̀ə _____

8. jə̌ _____   18. dǒ _____

9. ɔ̀ɔ _____   19. dùa _____

10. jùa _____   20. gìa _____

Lesson 3

colors; 'jǎ' (future tense); 'dâi' (can); more
vowels; complex vowels; final consonants;
ten vowels that change their forms;
tone rules for middle consonants (cont.)

bŏt-tíi săam   ບົດທີ ສາມ   Lesson 3

kám-săp   ຄຳສັບ   Vocabulary

jă ຈະ		will
dâi ໄດ້		can
dtɛɛ ແຕ່		but
sâa ຊ້າ		slow
sâa-sâa ຊ້າໆ		slowly
wái ໄວ		quick, fast
wái-wái ໄວໆ		quickly, fast
ìik-tʉa-nʉng ອີກເທື່ອນີ່ງ		one more time
het ເຮັດ		to do, to make
kúa-gìn ຄົວກິນ		to cook
mak ມັກ		to like
gìn ກິນ		to eat[1]
dʉʉm ດື່ມ		to drink[2]
bəng ເບິ່ງ		to watch
wâo/bpàak ເວົ້າ/ປາກ		to speak
aan ອ່ານ		to read
kĭan ຂຽນ		to write
hían ຮຽນ		to study
sɔ̌ɔn ສອນ		to teach
het-wîak ເຮັດວຽກ		to work
nɔ́ɔn ນອນ		to sleep
dtʉʉn/dtʉʉn-nɔɔn ຕື່ນ/ຕື່ນນອນ		to wake up
bpài ໄປ		to go
máa ມາ		to come
bɔɔ ບໍ່		not
geng ເກັ່ງ		good at

nɔ̀i-nʉng	ໜ້ອຍໜຶ່ງ	a little
lót/lótyon	ລົດ /ລົດຍົນ	car
wat	ວັດ	temple
bòot	ໂບດ	church
dta-làat	ຕະຫລາດ	market
hóong-héem	ໂຮງແຮມ	hotel
hóong-ngáan	ໂຮງງານ	factory
hóong-sǐi-nee-mâa	ໂຮງຊີເນມາ	movie theater
hóong-hían	ໂຮງຮຽນ	school
hóong-mɔ̌ɔ	ໂຮງໝໍ	hospital
ta-náa-káan	ທະນາຄານ	bank
bpài-sa-nǐi	ໄປສະນີ	post office
ma-hǎa-wi-ta-yáa-lái		university
ມະຫາວິທະຍາໄລ		
dən-bìn	ເດີ່ນບິນ	airport
hâan-àa-hǎan	ຮ້ານອາຫານ	restaurant
àa-hǎan-waang	ອາຫານຫວ່າງ	snack
kɔ̌ɔng-wǎan	ຂອງຫວານ	dessert
nâm/nâam	ນ້ຳ	water
nâm-gɔ̂ɔn	ນ້ຳກ້ອນ	ice
nâm-màak-gìang	ນ້ຳໝາກກ້ຽງ	orange juice
gàa-fée	ກາເຟ	coffee
sáa	ຊາ	tea
bìa	ເບຍ	beer
kào	ເຂົ້າ	rice
mii/fǒə	ໝີ່ /ເຝີ	noodles
àa-hǎan	ອາຫານ	food
àa-hǎan láao	ອາຫານລາວ	Lao food
àa-hǎan fa-lang	ອາຫານຝຣັ່ງ	western food
àa-hǎan jiin	ອາຫານຈິນ	Chinese food

àa-hǎan nyii-bpùn ອາຫານຍີ່ປຸ່ນ	Japanese food
kào-sâo/ àa-hǎan-sâo ເຂົ້າເຊົ້າ / ອາຫານເຊົ້າ	breakfast
kào-tiang/àa-hǎan-tiang ເຂົ້າທ່ຽງ / ອາຫານທ່ຽງ	lunch
kào-lέεng/ àa-hǎan-lέεng ເຂົ້າແລງ / ອາຫານແລງ	dinner
gìn-kào ກິນເຂົ້າ	to have a meal[3]
sǐi ສີ	color[4]
sǐi dàm ສີດຳ	black
sǐi kǎao ສີຂາວ	white
sǐi dὲεng ສີແດງ	red
sǐi kǐao ສີຂຽວ	green
sǐi fâa ສີຟ້າ	light blue
sǐi fâa-gεε ສີຟ້າແກ່	dark blue
sǐi nâm-dtàan ສີນ້ຳຕານ	brown
sǐi lǔang ສີເຫລືອງ	yellow
sǐi bùa ສີບົວ	pink
sǐi muang ສີມ່ວງ	purple
sǐi sεεt/sǐi sòm ສີແສດ / ສີສົ້ມ	orange
sǐi kìi-tao ສີຂີ້ເທົ່າ	grey

1. táan (ທານ – to eat) is a polite form of gìn (ກິນ – to eat).

2. Although duum (ດື່ມ) means to drink, Lao people tend to use gìn (ກິນ) in less formal speech for both 'eat' and 'drink'.
   e.g. kɔi mak gìn bìa. = I like to drink beer.

3. gìn-kào (ກິນເຂົ້າ) literally means "to eat rice". However, Lao people use this phrase for eating any main meal.

4. sǐi (ສີ) can be omitted when it is used to modify nouns.
   e.g. lot sǐi kǎao = lot kǎao (white car)

Conversation 1

Tongpet: jâo wâo páa-săa láao dâi bɔɔ.

ທອງເພັດ : ເຈົ້າ ເວົ້າ ພາສາ ລາວ ໄດ້ ບໍ?

     Can you speak Lao?

David: dâi nɔ̀i-nung.

ເດວິດ : ໄດ້ ໜ້ອຍໜຶ່ງ.

     Yes, a little.

Tongpet: jâo hían páa-săa láao yuu săi.

ທອງເພັດ : ເຈົ້າ ຮຽນ ພາສາ ລາວ ຢູ່ ໃສ?

     Where did you learn Lao?

David: kɔ̀i hían găp kón láao yuu àa-mée-li-gàa.

ເດວິດ : ຂ້ອຍ ຮຽນ ກັບ ຄົນ ລາວ ຢູ່ ອາເມລິກາ.

     With Lao people in America.

Tongpet: jâo wâo láao geng lăai.

ທອງເພັດ : ເຈົ້າ ເວົ້າ ລາວ ເກັ່ງ ຫລາຍ.

     You speak Lao very well.

David: kɔ̀ɔp-jai.

ເດວິດ : ຂອບໃຈ

     Thank you.

Note: wâo páa-săa láao or wâo láao = to speak Lao

Conversation 2

Mana: jâo mak gìn àa-hǎan láao bɔɔ.

ມານະ: ເຈົ້າ   ມັກ   ກິນ   ອາຫານ   ລາວ   ບໍ່?

    Do you like to eat Lao food?

Paul: mak laai.

ປອລ: ມັກ   ຫລາຍ.

    Yes, I like it very much.

    jâo mak àa-hǎan fa-lang bɔɔ.

    ເຈົ້າ ໍ ມັກ   ອາຫານ   ຝຣັ່ງ   ບໍ່?

    Do you like western food?

Mana: kɔi bɔɔ mak. kɔi mak àa-hǎan nyii-bpun.

ມານະ: ຂ້ອຍ   ບໍ່   ມັກ.   ຂ້ອຍ   ມັກ   ອາຫານ   ຍີ່ປຸ່ນ.

    No, I don't. I like Japanese food.

    jâo ja dùum sáa lúu-waa gàa-fée.

    ເຈົ້າ   ຈະ   ດຶ່ມ   ຊາ   ຫລືວ່າ   ກາເຟ?

    Will you drink tea or coffee?

Paul: ja dùum gàa-fée.

ປອລ: ຈະ   ດຶ່ມ   ກາເຟ.

    I will drink coffee.

bpà-nyòok   ปะໂຫຍກ   **Sentences**

1. A: jâo (bɔɔ) mak   àa-hǎan nyǎng.
       ເຈົ້າ (ບໍ່) ມັກ   ອາຫານ   ຫຍັງ?
       What food do (don't) you like?

    B: kɔ̀i (bɔɔ) mak àa-hǎan láao.
       ຂ້ອຍ (ບໍ່) ມັກ   ອາຫານ   ລາວ.
       I (don't) like Lao food.

    C: jâo (bɔɔ) mak sǐi nyǎng.
       ເຈົ້າ (ບໍ່)   ມັກ   ສີ   ຫຍັງ?
       What color do (don't) you like?

    D: kɔ̀i (bɔɔ) mak   sǐi kǎao.
       ຂ້ອຍ (ບໍ່)   ມັກ   ສີ ຂາວ.
       I (don't) like white.

    E: jâo (bɔɔ) mak het nyǎng.
       ເຈົ້າ (ບໍ່)   ມັກ   ເຮັດ ຫຍັງ?
       What do (don't) you like to do?

    F: kɔ̀i (bɔɔ) mak bəng tóo-la-tat.
       ຂ້ອຍ (ບໍ່)   ມັກ ເບິ່ງ ໂທລະຫັດ.
       I (don't) like watching T.V.

2. A: jâo mak àa-hǎan jìin bɔɔ.
       ເຈົ້າ ມັກ ອາຫານ   ຈິນ ບໍ່?
       Do you like Chinese food?

    B: mak.
       ມັກ.
       Yes, I do.

    C: bɔɔ mak.
       ບໍ່ ມັກ.
       No, I don't.

3. A: jâo maḳ àa-hǎan láao lɯɯ àa-hǎan fa-lang.
        ເຈົ້າ ມັກ ອາຫານ ລາວ ຫລື ອາຫານ ຝຣັ່ງ?
        Do you like Lao food or western food?

    B: kɔ̀i mak àa-hǎan láao.
        ຂ້ອຍ ມັກ ອາຫານ ລາວ.
        I like Lao food.

    C: jâo mak lot sǐi kǎao lɯɯ lot sǐi dὲεng.
        ເຈົ້າ ມັກ ລົດ ສີ ຂາວ ຫລື ລົດ ສີ ແດງ?
        Do you like white cars or red cars?

    D: kɔ̀i mak lot sǐi dὲεng.
        ຂ້ອຍ ມັກ ລົດ ສີ ແດງ.
        I like red cars.

4. A: jâo aan páa-sǎa láao dâi bɔɔ.
        ເຈົ້າ ອ່ານ ພາສາ ລາວ ໄດ້ ບໍ່?
        Can you read Lao?

    B: dâi.
        ໄດ້
        Yes, I can.

    C: bɔɔ dâi.
        ບໍ່ ໄດ້.
        No, I can't.

5. A: jâo kǐan páa-sǎa láao dâi bɔɔ.
        ເຈົ້າ ຂຽນ ພາສາ ລາວ ໄດ້ ບໍ່?
        Can you write in Lao?

    B: bɔɔ dâi. dtɛɛ aan dâi nɔ̀i-nɯng.
        ບໍ່ ໄດ້. ແຕ່ ອ່ານ ໄດ້ ໜ້ອຍໜຶ່ງ.
        No, I can't. But I can read a little.

6. A: jâo ja bpài sǎi.
        ເຈົ້າ ຈະ ໄປ ໃສ?
        Where will you go?

    B: jà bpài hâan-àa-hǎan láao.
        ຈະ ໄປ ຮ້ານອາຫານ ລາວ.
        I will go to a Lao restaurant.

C: ja bpài dən-bìn.

จะ ไป   ເດີ່ນບິນ.

I will go to the airport.

7.   A: láao mak dɯɯm nyăng.

ลาว   ມັກ   ດື່ມ   ຫຍັງ?

What does he/she like to drink?

B: láao mak dɯɯm gàa-fée.

ลาว   ມັກ   ດື່ມ   ກາເຝ.

He/she likes to drink coffee.

C: láao mak dɯɯm bia   láao.

ลาว   ມັກ   ດື່ມ   ເບຍ   ลาว.

He/she likes to drink Lao beer.

8.   A: jâo het wîak yuu săi.

ເຈົ້າ ເຮັດ ວຽກ ຢູ່ ໃສ?

Where do you work?

B: kɔi het wîak yuu wîang-jàn.

ຂ້ອຍ ເຮັດ ວຽກ   ຢູ່   ວຽງຈັນ.

I work in Vientian.

C: jâo ja gìn kào-tiang yuu săi.

ເຈົ້າ ຈະ ກິນ ເຂົ້າ–ທ່ຽງ ຢູ່ ໃສ?

Where will you have lunch?

D: yuu hân-àa-hăan láao.

ຢູ່   ຮ້ານອາຫານ   ลาว.

At a Lao restaurant.

9.   kɔ̌ɔ-tôot. wâo sâa-sâa dâi bɔɔ.

ຂໍ ໂທດ. ເວົ້າ ຊ້າໆ ໄດ້ ບໍ?

Excuse me. Could you speak slowly?

10.   wâo (kɯ́ɯn) ìik-tɯa-nɯng dâi bɔɔ.

ເວົ້າ (ຄືນ)   ອີກເທື່ອໜຶ່ງ ໄດ້ ບໍ?

Can you say that again?

Test 3

Match the English words with the Lao words.

_____ 1. school   a. wat   ວັດ

_____ 2. eat   b. sǐi dàm   ສີດຳ

_____ 3. airport   c. bəng   ເບິ່ງ

_____ 4. temple   d. sǐi kǎao   ສີຂາວ

_____ 5. to speak   e. lot   ລົດ

_____ 6. food   f. dən-bìn   ດິ່ນບິນ

_____ 7. black   g. sǐi dὲεng   ສີແດງ

_____ 8. rice   h. het   ເຮັດ

_____ 9. white   i. ma-hǎa-wi-ta-yáa-lái
                              ມະຫາວິທະຍາໄລ

_____ 10. tea   j. hóong-hían   ໂຮງຮຽນ

_____ 11. to watch   k. àa-hǎan-waang   ອາຫານຫວ່າງ

_____ 12. car   l. kào   ເຂົ້າ

_____ 13. to do, to make   m. àa-hǎan   ອາຫານ

_____ 14. university   n. gìn   ກິນ

_____ 15. snack   o. aan   ອ່ານ

                          p. sáa   ຊາ

                          q. wâo   ເວົ້າ

                          r. hóong-sǐi-nee-mâa   ໂຮງຊີເນມາ

Translate the following into English.

1. jâo het wîak yuu săi.

   ເຈົ້າ ເຮັດ ວຽກ ຢູ່ ໃສ?

   _____

2. kɔ̀i mak lot sĭi fâa.

   ຂ້ອຍ ມັກ ລົດ ສີ ຟ້າ.

   _____

3. jâo mak àa-hăan láao lɯ̆ɯ àa-hăan jìin.

   ເຈົ້າ ມັກ ອາຫານ ລາວ ຫລື ອາຫານ ຈີນ.

   _____

4. jâo jà bpai sai.

   ເຈົ້າ ຈະ ໄປ ໃສ?

   _____

5. jâo kĭan páa-săa láao dâi geng lăai.

   ເຈົ້າ ຂຽນ ພາສາ ລາວ ໄດ້ ເກັ່ງ ຫລາຍ.

   _____

More Vowels

The following vowels may sound either short or long (mostly short), but are categorized as long vowels for tone rule purposes.

−ำ   /àm/

ໄ−   /ài/ (mái-múan)

ໃ−   /ài/ (mái-má-lai)

ເ−ົາ   /ào/

ໄ− and ໃ− are pronounced the same. You need to memorize which one is used with a particular word.

Complex Vowels

The following can be considered complex vowels. They are vowels followed by the sonorant consonants ຍ or ວ and ອ .

−ໍຍ   /àai/

−ຽວ   /ìao/

ၢ—ၦ   /ìa/ is sometimes spelled ၢ—ၦ ၢ—ၟ .

—ၢၥ   /àao/

—ၥၦ   /ùai/

ၢ—ၥၦ   /u̇ai/

—ၥၦ   /ɔɔi/

ၟ—ၦ   /ooi/

—ၦ   /ui/

—ၥ   /iu/

ၢ—ၥ   /eeo/

ၢၢ—ၥ   /ɛɛo/

ၢ—ၦ   /əəi/

Practice Writing the Following Vowels

Use ອ /-/ as the consonant when practicing the following vowels.

ອຳ   ອ   ອ

ໃອ   ອ   ອ

ອາຍ   ອ   ອ

ອຽວ   ອ   ອ

ອາວ   ອ   ອ

ອວຍ   ອ   ອ

ເຈື້ຍ ເຈຍ ເຈຍ

ຈຈຍ ຈຍ ຈຍ

ໂຈຍ ໂຈ ໂຈ

ຈຸຍ ຈຍ ຈຍ

ຈິວ ຈວ ຈວ

ເຈວ ເຈວ ເຈວ

ແຈວ ແຈ ແຈ

ເຈື້ຍ ເຈຍ ເຈຍ

Read The Following Aloud

1. ກຳ ໃກ ໄກ ເກົາ ເກັຍ

2. ຈຳ ໃຈ ໄຈ ເຈົາ ເຈັຍ

3. ຄຳ ໃຄ ໄຄ ເຄົາ ເຄັຍ

4. ຕຳ ໃຕ ໄຕ ເຕົາ ເຕັຍ

5. ບຳ ໃບ ໄບ ເບົາ ເບັຍ

6. ປຳ ໃປ ໄປ ເປົາ ເປັຍ

7. ຊຳ ໃຊ ໄຊ ເຊົາ ເຊັຍ

8. ກຳ ກ່ຳ ກ້ຳ

9. ໃຈ ໃຈ່ ໃຈ້

10. ໄກ ໄກ່ ໄກ້

11. ເກົາ ເກົ່າ ເກົ້າ

12. ເບັຍ ເບັຍ ເບັ້ຍ

Final Consonants

There are eight final consonant sounds which can end a syllable. They are divided into two categories - sonorant and stop. Sonorant finals are voiced - if you touch your larynx (voice box) while pronouncing them, you will feel a vibration. Stop finals are unvoiced. The five sonorant and three stop finals are most commonly written as follows:

Sonorant Finals (All Low Consonants)

ງ	ງ ງົວ	ngóɔ ngúa (cow)	/ng/
ນ	ນ ນົກ	nɔ́ɔ nok (bird)	/n/
ມ	ມ ແມວ	mɔ́ɔ méɛo (cat)	/m/
ຍ	ຍ ຍູງ	yɔ́ɔ yúng (mosquito)	/ny/
ວ	ວ ວີ	wɔ́ɔ wíi (fan)	/w/

Stop Finals (All Mid Consonants)

ກ	ກ ໄກ່	gɔ̀ɔ gai (chicken)	/k/
ດ	ດ ເດັກ	dɔ̀ɔ dĕk (child)	/t/
ບ	ບ ແບ້	bɔ̀ɔ bɛ̂ɛ (goat)	/p/

Notes: 1. When ກ , ດ, ບ and ຍ are initial consonants, they are transcribed
        as /g-/, /d-/, /b-/ and /ny-/ respectively. However, when they are final
        consonants, they are transcribed as /-k/, /-t/, /-p/ and /-i/.
    2. ວ forms part of the vowels −ວ and ◌ົວ, which are transcribed as /àao/
        and /ùa/ respectively. ◌ິວ is transcribed as /iu/ and −ຽວ is tran-
        scribed as /iao/.

Practice Writing the
Following Consonants

The following consonants are written with one stroke.
Start near the ❶.

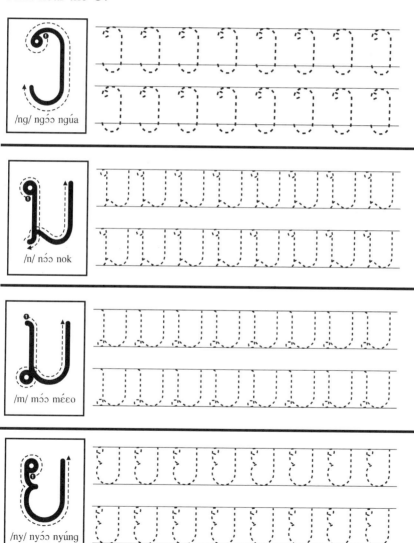

 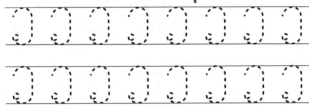

/w/ wɔ́ɔ wǐi

<u>Ten Vowels That Change Their Forms</u>

The following ten vowels change their forms when they appear in medial position.

Simple Vowels

Vowels	Final Position	Medial Position
◌ະ	ກະ /gǎ/	ກັດ /gǎt/
ເ◌ະ	ເປະ /bpě/	ເປັນ /bpèn/
ແ◌ະ	ແຕະ /dě/	ແຕກ /dtěk/
ໂ◌ະ	ໂຈະ /jǒ/	ຈົບ /jǒp/
ເ◌າະ	ເກາະ /gǒ/	ກ້ອບ /gɔ̌p/
◌ໍ	ສໍ /sɔ̌/	ສອນ /sɔ̌ɔn/

Diphthongs

Vowels	Final Position	Medial Position
ເ◌ັຍະ	ເຈັຍະ /jĭa/	ຈັຽກ /jĭak/
ເ◌ັຍ	ເສັຍ /sĭa/	ສັຽນ /sĭan/
◌ົວະ	ຕົວະ /dtŭa/	ຕົວນ /dtŭan/
◌ົວ	ມົວ /múa/	ມວນ /múan/

Special Vowel Alternatives

In the old Lao writing system, you may encounter some of the following alternative forms of these special vowels.

ໄ◌	/ài/	↔	◌ັຍ	/ài/
ໃ◌	/ài/	↔	◌ັຍ	/ài/
◌ໍາ	/àm/	↔	◌ັມ	/àm/

Live and Dead Syllables

To review, here are the rules for live and dead syllables:

A syllable that ends with a short vowel or a stop final consonant is called a <u>dead syllable</u>.

A syllable that ends with a long vowel or a sonorant final consonant is called a <u>live syllable</u>.

Rising tone and its corresponding tone mark $\left(\stackrel{+}{-} \right)$ never occur with a dead syllable.

Tone Rules for Middle Consonants (cont.)

In the absence of a tone mark, the tone rules for middle consonants are as follows:

Middle Consonant with <u>Live Syllable = Low Tone</u>

Middle Consonant with <u>Dead Syllable = Rising Tone</u>

Examples:

Middle Consonant + Any Vowel + <u>Sonorant Final</u>
     = Low Tone

		<u>Sound Produced</u>	<u>Meaning</u>
ก + ◌ี + น	= กิน (gìn)	to eat
จ + ◌ึ + ง	= จึง (jùng)	therefore
ก + โ– + ย	= โดย (dooi)	by

Middle Consonant + Short Vowel + <u>Stop Final</u>
    = Rising Tone

	<u>Sound Produced</u>	<u>Meaning</u>
ກ + ະ + ບ	= ກັບ (găp)	with, and
ບ + ◌ + ດ	= ປິດ (bpĭt)	to close
ຈ + ◌ + ກ	= ຈັກ (jăk)	wet

Reading Exercise: <u>Read the Following Words and Practice</u>
<u>Writing Them in Lao. Also Identify the Tones.</u>

1. ແອວ waist

2. ແອບ to hide

3. ຕາມ to follow

4. ຈອດ to park

5. ອາບ to bathe

6. ເກີນ to exceed

7. ຈັດ to arrange

8. ຕົກ to fall

9. ຕາຍ to die

10. ຈົບ to be finished

11. ປົນ to mix

12. ບຸກ to invade

13. ຕຽງ bed

14. ບານ to blossom

Writing Exercise 3

Transcribe the following into Lao script. Notice that most of the vowels are in medial position and must change forms accordingly.

1. jàn _____

2. bpə̀ət _____

3. bàng _____

4. gùam _____

5. jʉ̀ʉt _____

6. dtèm _____

7. pǒm _____

8. dàng _____

9. gěp _____

10. dǒk _____

11. dòn _____

12. èn _____

13. dèm _____

14. jʉ̀ng _____

15. bùam _____

16. òng _____

17. dèen _____

18. jěp _____

19. bpùat _____

20. bùak _____

Transcribe the following into Lao script using appropriate tone marks.

21. gân _____   31. dtǎn _____

22. jom _____   32. bìip _____

23. bâng _____   33. dâng _____

24. ùut _____   34. bǎt _____

25. gûng _____   35. bàai _____

26. jàam _____   36. oong _____

27. gao _____   37. jǎa _____

28. dtɯɯn _____   38. jèp _____

29. dâam _____   39. gὲεp _____

30. ôok _____   40. jǎao _____

Lesson 4

telling time; high consonants; tone rules for high consonants

bŏt-tíi sii   ບົດທີ ສີ່   Lesson 4

kám-săp   ຄຳສັບ   Vocabulary

wée-láa ເວລາ	time	
sua-móong ຊົ່ວໂມງ	hour	
náa-tíi ນາທີ	minute	
wi-náa-tíi ວິນາທີ	second	
dtòng/gòng ຕົງ/ກົງ	exactly	
kəng ເຄິ່ງ	half	
gùap ເກືອບ	almost	
bpàai ປາຍ	past	
lέεo ແລ້ວ	already	
bpa-máan ປະມານ	about	
ìik ອິກ	more, again	
ìik hàa náa-tíi ອິກຫ້ານາທີ	five more minutes	
sâa ຊ້າ	slow	
wái/sâo ໄວ/ເຊົ້າ	fast, early	
sŭai ສວຍ	late	
gɔɔn ກ່ອນ	before	
lăng ຫລັງ	after	
dtɔ̀ɔn ຕອນ	at	
dtɔ̀ɔn sâo ຕອນເຊົ້າ	in the morning	
dtɔ̀ɔn sŭai ຕອນສວຍ	late morning	
dtɔ̀ɔn tiang ຕອນທ່ຽງ	at noon	
dtɔ̀ɔn baai ຕອນບ່າຍ	in the afternoon	
dtɔ̀ɔn lέεng ຕອນແລງ	in the evening	
dtɔ̀ɔn kam ຕອນຄຳ	at night	
dtɔ̀ɔn dŏk ຕອນດຶກ	late at night	
dĭao-nîi/dtɔ̀ɔn nîi ດຽວນີ້/ຕອນນີ້	now	
waang-gîi-nîi ຫວ່າງກີ້ນີ້	just now	

nyáam-dai ຍາມໃດ   when
jàak/dtɛɛ ຈາກ/ແຕ່   from
tǎng/hǎa/hɔ̀ɔt ເຖິງ/ຫາ/ຮອດ   to, until

wée-láa   ເວລາ   **Time**

jǎk móong (lɛ̂ɛo)   What time is it?
ຈັກໂມງ (ແລ້ວ)?

a.m.   1:00   nɯng móong   ໜຶ່ງໂມງ
          2:00   sɔ̌ɔng móong   ສອງໂມງ
          3:00   sǎam móong   ສາມໂມງ
          4:00   sii móong   ສີໂມງ
          5:00   hàa móong   ຫ້າໂມງ
          6:00   hǒk móong (sâo)   ຫົກໂມງ (ເຊົ້າ)
          7:00   jět móong (sâo)   ເຈັດໂມງ (ເຊົ້າ)
          8:00   bpɛ̀ɛt móong (sâo)   ແປດໂມງ (ເຊົ້າ)
          9:00   gâo móong (sâo)   ເກົ້າໂມງ (ເຊົ້າ)
         10:00   sǐp móong (sâo)   ສິບໂມງ (ເຊົ້າ)
         11:00   sǐp-ět móong (sâo)   ສິບເອັດໂມງ (ເຊົ້າ)

p.m.   12:00   tiang/tiang-dtòng/sĭp sɔ̌ɔng móong

ທ່ຽງ / ທ່ຽງຕົງ / ສິບສອງໂມງ

1:00   baai nɯng (móong)/baai móong

ບ່າຍໝື່ງ (ໂມງ) / ບ່າຍໂມງ

2:00   (baai) sɔ̌ɔng móong   (ບ່າຍ) ສອງໂມງ

3:00   (baai) sǎam móong   (ບ່າຍ) ສາມໂມງ

4:00   (baai) sìi móong

(ບ່າຍ) ສີ່ໂມງ

5:00   (baai) hàa móong   (ບ່າຍ) ຫ້າໂມງ

6:00   hŏk móong (léɛng)   ຫົກໂມງ (ແລງ)

7:00   jĕt móong   ເຈັດໂມງ (ແລງ)

8:00   bpɛ̀ɛt móong   ແປດໂມງ (ແລງ)

9:00   gâo móong   ເກົ້າໂມງ (ແລງ)

10:00   sĭp móong   ສິບໂມງ (ແລງ)

11:00   sĭp ĕt móong   ສິບເອັດໂມງ (ແລງ)

a.m.   12:00   sĭp sɔ̌ɔng móong gang kɯɯn/tîang-kɯɯn

ສິບສອງໂມງກາງຄືນ/ ທ່ຽງຄືນ

Conversation

Kampong: jâo dtɯɯn jǎk móong.

ຄຳພົງ: ເຈົ້າ ຕື່ນ ຈັກ ໂມງ?

   What time do you get up?

Pakong: bpa-máan jět móong sâo.

ປະຄອງ: ປະມານ ເຈັດ ໂມງ ເຊົ້າ.

   About seven o'clock.

Kampong: gɔɔn bpài gàan jao het nyang dɛɛ.

ຄຳພົງ: ກ່ອນ ໄປ ການ ເຈົ້າ ເຮັດ ຫຍັງ ແດ່?

   What do you do before going to work?

Pakong: kɔi gìn kào sâo lɛ aan nǎng-sɯɯ-pím.

ປະຄອງ: ຂ້ອຍ ກິນ ເຂົ້າ ເຊົ້າ ແລະ ອ່ານ   ໜັງສືພິມ.

   I make breakfast and read the paper.

Kampong: jâo nɔɔn jǎk móong.

ຄຳພົງ: ເຈົ້າ ນອນ ຈັກ ໂມງ?

   What time do you go to bed?

Pakong: gàai tiang-kɯɯn bpài nɔi-nɯng.

ປະຄອງ: ກາຍ   ທ່ຽງຄືນ   ໄປ ໜ້ອຍໜຶ່ງ.

   A little after midnight.

bpà-nyòok   ปะโทยภ   **Sentences**

1. A: dtɔ̀ɔn nîi jăk móong (léɛo).

ຕອນ ນີ້ ຈັກ ໂມງ (ແລ້ວ) ?

What time is it now?

B: dtɔ̀ɔn nîi baai hàa móong.

ຕອນ ນີ້ ບ່າຍ ຫ້າ ໂມງ .

It's now five p.m.

C: dtɔ̀ɔn nîi tiang kəng.

ຕອນ ນີ້ ທ່ງງ ເຄິ່ງ .

It's now half past twelve noon.

D: dtɔ̀ɔn nîi gâao móong bpàai nɔ̀i-nɯng.

ຕອນ ນີ້ ເກົ້າ ໂມງ ປາຍ ໝ້ອຍໜຶ່ງ .

It's now a little past nine a.m.

E: dtɔ̀ɔn nîi baai sɔ̌ɔng móong dtòng.

ຕອນ ນີ້ ບ່າຍ ສອງ ໂມງ ຕົງ .

It's now exactly two p.m.

F: dtɔ̀ɔn nîi sǎam móong bpàai sǐp.

ຕອນ ນີ້ ສາມ ໂມງ ປາຍ ສິບ .

It's now ten minutes after three p.m.

G: dtɔ̀ɔn nîi sǐp ĕt móong saao.

ຕອນ ນີ້ ສິບ ເອັດ ໂມງ ຊາວ .

It's now twenty past eleven p.m.

H: dtɔ̀ɔn nîi nɯng móong kəng.

ຕອນ ນີ້ ໜຶ່ງ ໂມງ ເຄິ່ງ .

It's now half past one a.m.

2. A: jâo gìn kào lέεng jăk móong.

   ເຈົ້າ ກິນ ເຂົ້າ ແລງ ຈັກ ໂມງ?

   What time do you eat dinner?

B: kɔ̀i gìn kào lέεng (dtɔ̀ɔn)* hŏk móong.

   ຂ້ອຍ ກິນ ເຂົ້າ ແລງ (ຕອນ) ຫົກ ໂມງ.

   I eat dinner at six.

C: jâo bpài wîak jăk móong.

   ເຈົ້າ ໄປ ວຽກ ຈັກ ໂມງ?

   What time do you go to work?

D: kɔ̀i bpài wîak (dtɔ̀ɔn)* bpὲεt móong.

   ຂ້ອຍ ໄປ ວຽກ (ຕອນ) ແປດ ໂມງ.

   I go to work at eight.

E: jâo jă bəng tóo-la-tat jăk móong.

   ເຈົ້າ ຈະ ເບິ່ງ ໂທລະທັດ ຈັກ ໂມງ?

   What time will you watch T.V.?

F: kɔ̀i jă bəng tóo-la-tat dtɔ̀ɔn dŏk.

   ຂ້ອຍ ຈະ ເບິ່ງ ໂທລະທັດ ຕອນ ດຶກ.

   I will watch T.V. late at night.

   * dtɔ̀ɔn can be omitted in these sentences.

3. A: hàa móong dtong.

   ຫ້າ ໂມງ ຕົງ.

   Exactly 5 p.m.

B: hàa móong bpàai.

   ຫ້າ ໂມງ ປາຍ.

   Past 5 p.m.

C: hàa móong lέεng lêεo.

   ຫ້າ ໂມງ ແລງ ແລ້ວ.

   Already 5 p.m.

D: bpa-máan hàa móong.

ປະມານ   ຫ້າ   ໂມງ

Around 5 p.m.

E: gùap hàa móong.

ເກືອບ   ຫ້າ   ໂມງ

Almost 5 p.m.

F: hàa móong nyáng sǐp.

ຫ້າ   ໂມງ   ຍັງ   ສິບ.

Ten minutes to 5 p.m.

G: hàa móong bpàai hàa náa-tíi.

ຫ້າ   ໂມງ   ປາຍ   ຫ້າ   ນາທີ.

Five minutes past 5 p.m.

H: hàa móong bpàai sǐp.

ຫ້າ   ໂມງ   ປາຍ   ສິບ.

Ten past 5 p.m.

I: hàa móong kəng.

ຫ້າ   ໂມງ   ເຄິ່ງ.

Half past 5 p.m.

4.   A: láao máa sâa-sâa.

ລາວ   ມາ   ຊ້າໆ.

He came slowly.

B: láao máa wái.

ລາວ   ມາ   ໄວ.

He came early.

C: láao máa sǔai.

ລາວ   ມາ   ສວຍ.

He came late.

5. kɔ̀i hían páa-sǎa láao dtɛɛ baai móong tǔng baai sii móong.

    ຂ້ອຍ ຮຽນ ພາສາ   ລາວ ແຕ່ ບ່າຍ ໂມງ ເຖິງ ບ່າຍ ສີ່ ໂມງ.

    I study Lao from one p.m to four p.m.

6. A: jâo hían páa-sǎa láao jǎk sua-móong.

    ເຈົ້າ ຮຽນ   ພາສາ ລາວ ຈັກ ຂົ້ວໂມງ?

    How many hours do you study Lao?

    B: kɔ̀i hían páa-sǎa láao sǎam sua-móong.

    ຂ້ອຍ ຮຽນ   ພາສາ ລາວ   ສາມ   ຂົ້ວໂມງ.

    We study Lao for three hours.

7. A: jâo lə̂əm aan bpûm dtɛɛ dtɔɔn jǎk móong.

    ເຈົ້າ ເລີ້ມ ອ່ານ ປື້ມ   ແຕ່ ຕອນ ຈັກ ໂມງ?

    When did you start reading?

    B: kɔ̀i lə̂m aan bpûm dtɛɛ dtɔɔn gâo móong lɛ́ɛng.

    ຂ້ອຍ ເລີ້ມ ອ່ານ ປື້ມ   ແຕ່   ຕອນ ເກົ້າ   ໂມງ ແລງ.

    I've been reading since nine p.m.

    aan bpûm literally means " to read a book". It also
    means "to read" in general.

8. láao ja bpài dən-bìn dtɔɔn baai sǎam móong.

    ລາວ ຈະ ໄປ ເດີ່ນ-ບິນ ຕອນ ບ່າຍ ສາມ ໂມງ.

    He will go to the airport at three p.m.

9. dtɔɔn tiang kɔ̀i ja het àa hǎan láao.

    ຕອນ ທ່ຽງ ຂ້ອຍ ຈະ ເຮັດ ອາຫານ ລາວ.

    I will make Lao food at noon.

10. kɔ̀i ja bpài hɔ̀ng-nâm hàa náa-tíi.

    ຂ້ອຍ ຈະ ໄປ   ຫ້ອງນ້ຳ   ຫ້າ ນາທີ.

    I will go to the bathroom for five minutes.

11. kɔ̀i het wîak hàa sua-móong kəng.

    ຂ້ອຍ ເຮັດ ວຽກ ຫ້າ   ຂົ້ວໂມງ ເຄິ່ງ.

    I work for five and a half hours.

12.   ìik sǐp náa-tíi kɔ̀i ja tóo máa hǎa jâo.

       ອິກ ສິບ ນາທີ ຂ້ອຍ ຈະ ໂທ ມາ ຫາ ເຈົ້າ.

       I will give you a call in ten minutes.

13.   kɔ̀i het-wîak dtɛɛ sâo hɔ̀ɔt tiang.

       ຂ້ອຍ ເຮັດວຽກ ແຕ່ ເຊົ້າ ຣອດ ທ່ຽງ.

       I work from morning till noon.

14. A: jâo ja bpài ta-náa-káan nyáam dǎi.

       ເຈົ້າ ຈະ ໄປ ທະນາຄານ ຍາມ ໃດ?

       When will you go to the bank?

    B: dtɔ̀ɔn baai.

       ຕອນ ບ່າຍ.

       In the afternoon.

Test 4

Tell what time it is indicating a.m. or p.m. (Use either a.m or p.m., but if you want to write both when there is more than one answer, that's fine also.) Look at the example.

Example: sǎam móong =   3:00 p.m./3:a.m.

1. hǒk móong sǐp hàa. ຫົກໂມງສິບຫ້າ _____

2. baai sǎam. ບ່າຍສາມ _____

3. sii móong kəng. ສີ່ໂມງເຄິ່ງ _____

4. sɔ̌ɔng móong sǎam sǐp hàa. ສອງໂມງສິບຫ້າ. _____

5. baai sǎam móong gòng. ບ່າຍສາມໂມງກົງ. _____

6. hàa móong yáng sǐp. ຫ້າໂມງຍັງສິບ. _____

7. sǐp sɔ̌ɔng móong sáao. ສິບສອງໂມງຂາວ _____

8. baai nɯng móong hàa náa-tíi. ບ່າຍໜຶ່ງໂມງຫ້ານາທີ.

    _____

9. bpɛ̀ɛt móong sáao náa-tíi. ແປດໂມງຂາວນາທີ. _____

10. sii móong sâo. ສີ່ໂມງເຊົ້າ _____

11. sǐp móong sâo. ສິບໂມງເຊົ້າ _____

12. tiang dtòng. ທ່ຽງຕົງ _____

13. bpɛ̀ɛt móong lɛ́ɛng. ແປດໂມງແລງ _____

14. bpɛ̀ɛt móong sǐp. ແປດໂມງສິບ _____

15. hàa móong sâo. ຫ້າໂມງເຊົ້າ _____

Translate the following into English.

1. kɔ̌i   sì bpài   wat dtɔɔn tiang.
    ຂ້ອຍ ສິ ໄປ   ວັດ   ຕອນ ທ່ຽງ.

---

2. láao aan bpûm dtâng-dtɛɛ sǐp-et móong lɛ́ɛng.
    ລາວ ອ່ານ ປື້ມ ຕັ້ງແຕ່   ສິບເອັດ ໂມງ   ແລງ.

---

3. háo hían páa-sǎa láao sǎam sua-móong.
    ເຮົາ ຮຽນ ພາສາ   ລາວ ສາມ ຊົ່ວໂມງ.

---

4. dtɔ̀ɔn nîi wée-láa baai móong kəng.
    ຕອນ   ນີ້ ເວລາ   ບ່າຍ ໂມງ ເຄິ່ງ.

---

5. kɔ̌i gìn kào-sâo dtɔ̀ɔn bpɛ̀ɛt móong.
    ຂ້ອຍ ກິນ ເຂົ້າເຊົ້າ   ຕອນ ແປດ ໂມງ.

High Consonants

ອັກສອນສູງ (ăk-sɔ̌ɔn-sǔung)

There are six "high" consonants in Lao as follows:

Consonant		Consonant Name	Sound
ຂ	ຂ ໄຂ່	kɔ̌ɔ kai - egg	/k/
ສ	ສ ເສືອ	sɔ̌ɔ sǔa - tiger	/s/
ຖ	ຖ ຖົງ	tɔ̌ɔ tǒng - bag	/t/
ຜ	ຜ ເຜິ້ງ	pɔ̌ɔ pèng - bee	/p/
ຝ	ຝ ຝົນ	fɔ̌ɔ fǒn - rain	/f/
ຫ	ຫ ຫ່ານ	hɔ̌ɔ haan - goose	/h/

Practice Writing the High Consonants

Notice that you always start with a small circle where there is one. Start near the ❶.

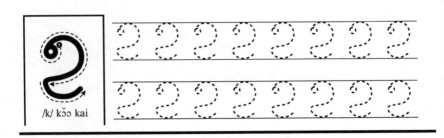

/k/ kɔ̌ɔ kai

/s/ sŏɔ sŭa

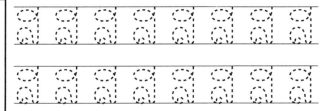

/t/ tɔ̌ɔ tŏng

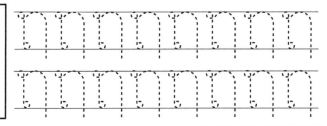

/p/ pɔ̌ɔ pɛ̀ng

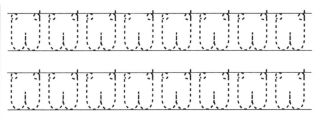

/f/ fɔ̌ɔ fŏn

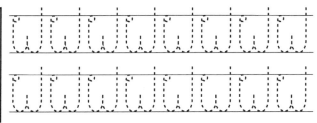

/h/ hɔ̌ɔ haan

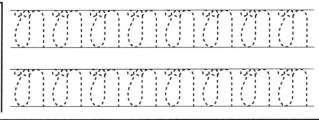

Tone Rules for High Consonants

In the absence of a tone mark, the tone rules for high consonants are as follows:

High Consonant with Live Syllable = Rising Tone

High Consonant with Dead Syllable = Rising or Low Tone

Examples:

High Consonant + Long Vowel = Rising Tone

		Sound Produced	Meaning
ຂ + − า	=	ຂາ (kǎa)	leg
ຜ + ◌ີ	=	ຜີ (pǐi)	ghost
ເ + ເ◌ົา	=	ເສົາ (sǎo)	mast

Reading Exercise: <u>Read the Following Words and Practice Writing Them in Lao.</u>

1. ຫົວ head   2. ເສືອ tiger

3. ໄຝ mole   4. ຫູ ear

5. ແຂນ arm   6. ຜົວ husband

7. ສີ color   8. ຫາ to look for

9. ຝາ lid   10. ສາມ three

High Consonant + Short Vowel = Rising Tone

	<u>Sound Produced</u>	<u>Meaning</u>

ສ + −ະ   = ສະ (sǎ)   pond

ຫ + ເ−າະ   = ເຫາະ (hǒ)   to fly e.g. superman

Reading Exercise: <u>Read the Following Words and Practice Writing Them in Lao.</u>

1. ຝຸ rotten

2. ສະຫະ united

3. ສີວະ name of a god, mountain (Sanskrit)

High Consonant + Any Vowel + <u>Sonorant Final</u> = Rising Tone

	Sound Produced	Meaning

ຂ + ◌ั + ມ = ຂັມ (kǎn)   to crow, to coo

ສ + −າ + ມ = ສາມ (sǎam)   three

ຖ + ◌ັ + ງ = ຖົງ (tǒng)   sack

High Consonant + Short Vowel + <u>Stop Final</u> = Rising Tone

	Sound Produced	Meaning

ຂ + ◌ั + ບ = ຂັບ (kǎp)   to drive

ຜ + ◌ិ + ດ = ຜິດ (pǐt)   wrong

ຖ + ◌ຶ + ກ = ຖືກ (tǔuk)   correct

High Consonant + Long Vowel + <u>Stop Final</u> = Low Tone

	Sound Produced	Meaning

ຜ + −າ + ກ = ຜາກ (fàak)   to deposit

ສ + ◌ູ + ບ = ສູບ (sùup)   to smoke

ຫ + ໂ− + ດ = ໂຫດ (hòot)   cruel

Reading Exercise: Read the Following Words and Practice
Writing Them in Lao. Also Identify the Tones.

1. ສູງ tall   2. ເຖິງ to

3. ຫາດ beach   4. ຜົມ hair

5. ສຸກ ripe   6. ແຂກ guest

7. ຫົກ six   8. ຖານ base

9. ເຂີຍ son-in-law 10. ສິບ ten

11. ສາຍ line   12. ຂັງ to detain

Writing Exercise 4

Transcribe the following into Lao script.

1. sǎa _____   8. hǔp _____

2. pǎ _____   9. tǔng _____

3. sàak _____   10. pǒng _____

4. kùut _____   11. fǎn _____

5. sǐao _____   12. hàap _____

6. fǐi _____   13. fàat _____

7. hὲεk _____   14. fǔung _____

Lesson 5

days of the week; months; tone marks with high consonants; low consonants introduced

bŏt-tíi hàa   ບົດທິ ຫ້າ   Lesson 5

kám-săp   ຄຳສັບ   Vocabulary

wán	ວັນ	day
wán-àa-tit	ວັນອາທິດ	Sunday[1]
wán-jàn	ວັນຈັນ	Monday
wán-àng-káan	ວັນອັງຄານ	Tuesday
wán-put	ວັນພຸດ	Wednesday
wán-pa-hăt	ວັນພະຫັດ	Thursday
wán-sŭk	ວັນສຸກ	Friday
wán-săo	ວັນເສົາ	Saturday
wán-pak	ວັນພັກ	holiday
săo-àa-tit	ເສົາອາທິດ	weekend
dŭan	ເດືອນ	month
máng-gɔ̀ɔn	ມັງກອນ	January[2]
gùm-páa	ກຸມພາ	February
míi-náa	ມີນາ	March
mée-săa	ເມສາ	April
pɯt-sà-paa	ພຶດສະພາ	May
mì-tù-náa	ມິຖຸນາ	June
gɔɔ-la-got	ກໍລະກົດ	July
sĭng-hăa	ສິງຫາ	August
gàn-nyáa	ກັນຍາ	September
dtù-láa	ຕຸລາ	October
pa-jĭk	ພະຈິກ	November
tán-wáa	ທັນວາ	December
mûu-nîi	ມື້ນີ້	today
mûu-wáan-nîi	ມື້ວານນີ້	yesterday

mûu-ʉʉn	ມື້ອື່ນ	tomorrow
tuk/tuk-tuk	ທຸກ/ທຸກໆ	every
sɔ̌ɔng mûu gɔɔn	ສອງມື້ກ່ອນ	two days ago
sǎam mûu gɔɔn	ສາມມື້ກ່ອນ	three days ago
ìik sɔ̌ɔng mûu	ອີກສອງມື້	two days from now
ìik sǎam mûu	ອີກສາມມື້	three days from now
tuk-tuk mûu	ທຸກໆມື້	everyday
àa-tit/sǎp-pa-dàa	ອາທິດ/ສັບປະດາ	week[1]
àa-tit-nîi	ອາທິດນີ້	this week
àa-tít gɔ̀ɔn/àa-tit-lɛ̂ɛo	ອາທິດກ່ອນ/ອາທິດແລ້ວ	last week
sɔ̌ɔng àa-tit gɔɔn ສອງອາທິດກ່ອນ		two weeks ago
sǎam àa-tit gɔɔn ສາມອາທິດກ່ອນ		three weeks ago
ìik sɔ̌ɔng àa-tit	ອີກສອງອາທິດ	two weeks from now
ìik sǎam àa-tit	–ອີກສາມອາທິດ	three weeks from now
tuk-tuk àa-tit	ທຸກໆອາທິດ	every week
dʉan-nîi	ເດືອນນີ້	this month
dʉan-lɛ̂ɛo	ເດືອນແລ້ວ	last month
dʉan-nàa	ເດືອນໜ້າ	next month
sɔ̌ɔng dʉan gɔɔn ສອງເດືອນກ່ອນ		two months ago
sǎam dʉan gɔ̀ɔn ສາມເດືອນກ່ອນ		three months ago
ìik sɔ̌ɔng dʉan	ອີກສອງເດືອນ	two months from now

'iik sǎam dừan   ອີກສາມເຄືອນ   three months from now

tuk-tuk dừan   ທຸກໆເຄືອນ   every month

bpìi   ປີ   year

bpìi-nîi   ປີນີ້   this year

bpìi-gàai/bpìi lέεo   ປີກາຍ /ປີແລ້ວ   last year

bpìi-nàa   ປີໜ້າ   next year

sɔ̌ɔng bpìi gɔɔn   ສອງປີກ່ອນ   two years ago

'iik sɔ̌ɔng bpìi   ອີກສອງປີ   two years from now

tuk-tuk bpìi   ທຸກໆປີ   every year

dtɔ̀ɔn/mừu sâo   ຕອນ /ມື້ເຊົ້າ   morning

(mừu) sâo-nîi   (ມື້) ເຊົ້ານີ້   this morning

mừu-ừun sâo   ມື້ອື່ນເຊົ້າ   tomorrow morning

sâo-wán àa-tit   ເຊົ້າວັນອາທິດ   Sunday morning

tuk-tuk sâo   ທຸກໆເຊົ້າ   every morning

dtɔ̀ɔn/mừu lέεng   ຕອນ /ມື້ແລງ   evening

mừu-lέεng-nîi   ມື້ແລງນີ້   this evening

lέεng-wáan-nîi   ແລງວານນີ້   yesterday evening

mừu-ừun-lέεng   ມື້ອື່ນແລງ   tomorrow evening

lέεng wán-àa-tit   ແລງວັນອາທິດ   Sunday evening

tuk-tuk lέεng   ທຸກໆແລງ   every evening

gàang/kừun   ຄືນ   night

dtɔɔn-kam-mừu-nîi   ຕອນຄ່ຳມື້ນີ້   tonight

mừu-kừun-wáan-nîi   ມື້ຄືນວານນີ້   last night

kừun mừu-ừun   ຄືນມື້ອື່ນ   tomorrow night

kừun wán-àa-tit   ຄືນວັນອາທິດ   Sunday night

tuk-tuk kừun   ທຸກໆຄືນ   every night

kón hak ຄົນຮັກ	loved one
pûan/muu ເພື່ອນ/ໝູ່	friend
puu-baao ຜູ້ບ່າວ	boyfriend
puu-săao ຜູ້ສາວ	girlfriend
waang ຫວ່າງ	to have free time
nyùng ຫຍຸ້ງ	busy
dtɔ̂ng ຕ້ອງ	must
mîi ມີ	to have, there is/are
bpŭk ປຸກ	to wake someone up
mʉa/gắp/kʉʉn ເມືອ/ກັບ/ຄືນ	to return
bpài-tiao ໄປທ່ຽວ	to take a trip[3]
máa-hap ມາຮັບ	to come to pick up
bpài-hap ໄປຮັບ	to go to pick up
dtɛ̀ɛ-sâo ແຕ່ເຊົ້າ	early morning
dǒk ດຶກ	late at night
gắp/nám-gàn ກັບ/ນຳກັນ	and, together with
bpai nám-gàn ໄປນຳກັນ	to go together
kón-dìao/puu-dìao ຄົນດຽວ/ຜູ້ດຽວ	by oneself
mîi-nat ມີນັດ	have a date, appointment
pop-gàn-mai ພົບກັນໃໝ່	"see you again"
aa-lŏo ອັນໂຫລ	"hello" (on the phone)
ɔ̀o-kée ໂອເຄ	O.K.

1. àa-tit (ອາທິດ) means "week". Don't get it mixed up with
   wán-àa-tit (ວັນອາທິດ) which means "Sunday".
2. máng-gɔ̀ɔn (ມັງກອນ) is sometimes seen written as mok-ga-láa (ມົກກະລາ) .
3. bpài-tiao (ໄປທ່ຽວ) means to take a pleasure trip or to simply go out
   for pleasure.

Conversation

Tim: aa-lǒo.

ທິມ :   ອາໂຫລ

Hello.

Jambpaa: aa-lǒo. nîi mɛɛn jam-bpaa wâo.

ຈຳປາ: ອາໂຫລ.   ນີ້ ແມ່ນ   ຈຳປາ   ເວົ້າ.

Hello.   Jambpaa speaking.

Tim: sa-bàai-dìi jam-bpaa. nîi mɛɛn tím na.*

ທິມ: ສະບາຍດີ   ຈຳປາ.   ນີ້ ແມ່ນ ທິມ ນ່ະ.

Hi Jambpaa. It's Tim speaking.

Nit: sabàai dìi tim. jao sa-bàai dìi bɔɔ.

ຈຳປາ: ສະບາຍ ດີ ທິມ.   ເຈົ້າ ສະບາຍ ດີ ບໍ່?

Hi Tim. How are you?

Tim: kɔ̀i sa-bàai dìi. mûu-ùun lɛ́ɛng jâo waang bɔɔ.

ທິມ: ຂ້ອຍ ສະບາຍ ດີ.   ມື້ອື່ນ   ແລງ ເຈົ້າ ຫວ່າງ ບໍ່?

I'm fine. Are you free tomorrow night?

Nit: bɔɔ, kɔ̀i bɔɔ waang. mûu-ùun lɛɛng kɔ̀i dtông het wîak.

ຈຳປາ: ບໍ່, ຂ້ອຍ ບໍ່   ຫວ່າງ .   ມື້ອື່ນ ແລງ ຂ້ອຍ ຕ້ອງ ເຮັດ ວຽກ.

No, I'm not. I have to work tomorrow night.

Tim: lɛ̂ɛo wán-sǔk dee.

ທິມ: ແລ້ວ ວັນ ສຸກ ເດ?

What about Friday?

Nit: kúun wán-sǔk waang yuu.*

ຈຳປາ: ຄືນ ວັນ ສຸກ   ຫວ່າງ ຢູ່.

I'm free Friday night.

Tim: kɔ̀i ja bpài gìn àa-hǎan yii-bpun.

ທິມ: ຂ້ອຍ ຈະ ໄປ ກິນ ອາຫານ   ຍີ່ປຸ່ນ.

I will go eat out at a Japanese restaurant.

("na" and "yuu" is an ending particle used for emphasis.)

bpai nam-gan bɔɔ.

ໄປ   ນຳກັນ   ບໍ່?

Do you want to go with me?

Jambpaa: òo-kée. kɯ́ɯn wán-sŭk bpài dâi yuu.

ຈຳປາ :   ໂອ ເຄ.   ຄືນ   ວັນສຸກ   ໄປ   ໄດ້ ຢູ່.

O.K. I can go Friday night.

jâo ja bpài jăk móong.

ເຈົ້າ ຈະ ໄປ   ຈັກ   ໂມງ?

What time are you going?

Tim: bpa-máan bpɛ̀ɛt móong.

ທິມ :   ປະມານ   ແປດ   ໂມງ.

About eight o'clock.

kɔi ja bpài-hap jâo dtɔ̀ɔn hŏk móong kəng də́ə.

ຂ້ອຍ ຈະ ໄປຮັບ   ເຈົ້າ ຕອນ   ຫົກ   ໂມງ   ເຄິ່ງ ເດີ້.

("dəə" is an ending particle used for suggestion, persuasion or asking for

an agreement.)

I will go pick you up at half past six.

Jambpaa: kɔ̀ɔp-jai. lɛɛo pop gàn wán-sŭk dtɔ̀ɔn hŏk móong kəng.

ຈຳປາ :   ຂອບໃຈ.   ແລ້ວ ພົບ   ກັນ   ວັນສຸກ   ຕອນ   ຫົກ   ໂມງ   ເຄິ່ງ.

Thank you. See you Friday at half past six.

Tim: tɔɔ-nîi nɔ.

ທິມ :   ທໍ່ນີ້   ເນາະ.

Good-bye. (On the phone. Literally means "That's it".)

Jambpaa: sôok-dìi də́ə.

ຈຳປາ :   ໂຊກດີ   ເດີ້.

Good-luck.

bpà-nyòok   ປະໂຫຍກ   **Sentences**

1. A: mûu-nîi mɛɛn wán nyǎng.
    ມື້ນີ້   ແມ່ນ ວັນ ຫຍັງ?
    What day is today?

    B: mûu-nîi mɛɛn wán-àa-tit.
    ມື້ນີ້   ແມ່ນ ວັນອາທິດ.
    Today is Sunday.

2. A: mûu-ʉʉn mɛɛn wán nyǎng.
    ມື້ອື່ນ   ແມ່ນ ວັນ ຫຍັງ?
    What day is tomorrow?

    B: mûu-ʉʉn mɛɛn wán-jàn.
    ມື້ອື່ນ   ແມ່ນ ວັນຈັນ.
    Tomorrow is Monday.

3. A: dʉan nîi mɛɛn dʉan nyǎng.
    ເດືອນ ນີ້ ແມ່ນ ເດືອນ ຫຍັງ?
    What month is this?

    B: dʉan nîi mɛɛn dʉan míi-náa.
    ເດືອນ ນີ້ ແມ່ນ ເດືອນ   ມີນາ.
    This month is March.

4. A: bpìi nîi mɛɛn bpìi nyǎng.
    ປີ ນີ້ ແມ່ນ ປີ   ຫຍັງ?
    What year is this?

    B: bpìi nîi mɛɛn bpìi sɔ̌ɔng-pán-sǎam.
    ປີ   ນີ້ ແມ່ນ ປີ   ສອງພັນສາມ.
    This year is 2003.

5. A: mûu-nîi mɛɛn wán-tíi tao-dǎi.
    ມື້ນີ້   ແມ່ນ   ວັນທີ ເທົ່າໃດ?
    What is the date today?

    B: mûu-nîi mɛɛn wán-tíi sǐp-hàa.
    ມື້ນີ້   ແມ່ນ ວັນທີ ສິບຫ້າ.
    Today is the 15th.

C: mǔu-níi mɛɛn wán-tíi sǐp-hàa dùan mée-sǎa.

ມື້ນີ້   ແມ່ນ   ວັນທີ   ສິບຫ້າ   ເດືອນ   ເມສາ.

Today is April 15th.

D: mǔu-níi mɛɛn wán-sǎo tíi sǐp-hàa dùan mée-sǎa.

ມື້ນີ້   ແມ່ນ   ວັນເສົາ   ທີ   ສິບຫ້າ   ເດືອນ   ເມສາ.

Today is Saturday, April 15th.

6. A: jâo ja bpài mùang láao dùan dǎi.

ເຈົ້າ ຈະ ໄປ   ເມືອງ   ລາວ   ເດືອນ ໃດ?

What month are you going to Laos?

B: kòi ja bpài mùang láao dùan gàn-yáa.

ຂ້ອຍ ຈະ ໄປ   ເມືອງ   ລາວ   ເດືອນ   ກັນຍາ.

I will go to Laos in September.

7. A: jâo míi wán-pak mùa-dǎi.

ເຈົ້າ   ມີ   ວັນພັກ   ເມື່ອໃດ?

When do you have a holiday?

B: kòi míi wán-pak dùan nàa.

ຂ້ອຍ   ມີ   ວັນພັກ   ເດືອນ ໜ້າ.

I have a holiday next month.

8. A: wán-àa-tit nîi jâo ja het nyǎng.

ວັນອາທິດ   ນີ້ ເຈົ້າ ຈະ ເຣັດ ຫຍັງ?

What will you do this coming Sunday?

B: wán-àa-tit nîi kòi ja bpài gìn àa-hǎan láao.

ວັນອາທິດ   ນີ້ ຂ້ອຍ ຈະ ໄປ ກິນ ອາຫານ ລາວ.

This Sunday I will go to eat Lao food.

9. A: mǔu-kùun-wáan-nîi jâo het nyǎng.

ມື້ຄືນວານນີ້   ເຈົ້າ ເຣັດ ຫຍັງ?

What did you do last night?

B: kòi bpài gìn bìa gǎp muu.

ຂ້ອຍ ໄປ ກິນ ເບຍ ກັບ ໝູ່.

I went to drink beer with a friend.

10. A: láao yuu múang láao jǎk bpìi.
ลาว ยู่ เมือง ลาว จัก ปี?
How long was he in Laos?

B: láao yuu múang láao hàa bpìi.
ลาว ยู่ เมือง ลาว ท้า ปี.
He was in Laos for five years.

11. A: àa-tit nàa jâo ja het nyǎng.
ອາທິດ ໜ້າ ເຈົ້າ ຈະ ເຮັດ ຫຍັງ?
What will you do next week?

B: àa-tit nàa kɔ̀i ja bpai yii-bpun.
ອາທິດ ໜ້າ ຂ້ອຍ ຈະ ໄປ ຍີ່ປຸ່ນ.
Next week I will go to Japan.

12. múu-wáan-nìi kɔ̀i lóm tóo-ra-sǎp kəng sua-móong.
ມື້ວານນີ້ ຂ້ອຍ ລົມ ໂທລະສັບ ເຄິ່ງ ຊົ່ວໂມງ.
Yesterday I talked on the phone for half an hour.

13. kɔ̀i hían páa-sǎa láao tuk àa-tit.
ຂ້ອຍ ຮຽນ ພາສາ ລາວ ທຸກ ອາທິດ.
I study Lao every week.

14. kɔ̀i hían páa-sǎa láao tuk wán-àa-tit.
ຂ້ອຍ ຮຽນ ພາສາ ລາວ ທຸກ ວັນອາທິດ.
I study Lao every Sunday.

15. láao máa het wîak dtɛɛ dǎk.
ລາວ ມາ ເຮັດ ວຽກ ແຕ່ ດຶກ.
He comes to work early in the morning.

16. sǎo-àa-tit kɔ̀i mak dtɯɯn sǔai.
ເສົາອາທິດ ຂ້ອຍ ມັກ ຕື່ນ ສວຍ.
I like to wake up late on weekends.

17. A: pûak-jâo yuu múang-láao jǎk dɯan.
ພວກເຈົ້າ ຢູ່ ເມືອງລາວ ຈັກ ເດືອນ?
How many months were you in Laos?

B: pûak-háo yuu mɯ́ang-láao sǎam dɯ̀an.

ພວກເຮົາ ຢູ່ ເມືອງລາວ ສາມ ເດືອນ

We were in Laos for three months.

18.   pûak-háo yuu mɯ́ang-láao dtɛɛ dɯ̀an mi-tu-náa tɤ̌ng dɯan sǐng hǎa.

ພວກເຮົາ ຢູ່ ເມືອງລາວ ແຕ່ ເດືອນ ມິທຸນາ ເຖິງ ເດືອນ ສິງຫາ.

We were in Laos from June to August.

(The word "dɯ̀an" can be dropped in front of the month.)

19.   láao míi wée-láa waang tuk sǎo-àa-tit.

ລາວ ມີ ເວລາ ຫວ່າງ ທຸກ ເສົາອາທິດ.

He has free time every weekend.

20.   sɔ̌ɔng mɯ̀ɯ paan máa kɔ̀i bpài het wîak sǔai.

ສອງ ມື້ ຜ່ານ ມາ ຂ້ອຍ ໄປ ເຮັດ ວຽກ ສວຍ.

The last two days I went to work late.

21.   bpìi-nàa kɔ̀i ja hían páa-sǎa láao gǎp páa-sǎa jìin.

ປີ ຫນ້າ ຂ້ອຍ ຈະ ຮຽນ ພາສາ ລາວ ກັບ ພາສາ ຈີນ.

Next year I will study Lao and Chinese.

22.   àa-tit lɛ́ɛo kɔ̀i mɯa-bâan dɤ̌k tuk mɯ̀ɯ.

ອາທິດ ແລ້ວ ຂ້ອຍ ເມືອບ້ານ ເດິກ ທຸກ ມື້.

Last week I returned home late everyday.

23.   ìik sǎam bpìi kɔ̀i ja gǎp bpài mɯ́ang láao.

ອີກ ສາມ ປີ ຂ້ອຍ ຈະ ກັບ ໄປ ເມືອງ ລາວ.

I will return to Laos in three years.

24.   mɯ̀ɯ sáo-níi kɔ̀i gìn kâo kón dìao.

ມື້ ເຊົ້າ ນີ້ ຂ້ອຍ ກິນ ເຂົ້າ ຄົນ ດຽວ.

This morning I ate breakfast by myself.

25.   kɔ̀i míi-nat gǎp puu sǎao kɔ̀i tuk kɯ́ɯn wán-sǔk.

ຂ້ອຍ ມີ ນັດ ກັບ ຜູ້ ສາວ ຂ້ອຍ ທຸກ ຄືນ ວັນ ສຸກ.

I have a date with my girlfriend every Friday night.

Test 5

Match the English words with the Lao words.

Days ວັນ

_____ 1. Sunday	a. wán-pa-hăt ວັນພະຫັດ
_____ 2. Monday	b. wán-săo ວັນເສົາ
_____ 3. Tuesday	c. wán-àa-tit ວັນອາທິດ
_____ 4. Wednesday	d. wán-sŭk ວັນສຸກ
_____ 5. Thursday	e. wán-jàn ວັນຈັນ
_____ 6. Friday	f. wán-àng káan ວັນອັງຄານ
_____ 7. Saturday	g. wán-pak ວັນພັກ
_____ 8. holiday	h. wán-put ວັນພຸດ

Months ເດືອນ

_____ 1. January

a. mée-săa
ເມສາ

_____ 2. February

b. tán-wáa
ທັນວາ

_____ 3. March

c. sĭng-hăa
ສິງຫາ

_____ 4. April

d. pa-jik
ພະຈິກ

_____ 5. May

e. gùm-páa
ກຸມພາ

_____ 6. June

f. gàn-yáa
ກັນຍາ

_____ 7. July

g. pɯt-sà-páa
ພຶດສະພາ

_____ 8. August

h. mi-tù-náa
ມິຖຸນາ

_____ 9. September

i. máng-gɔɔn
ມັງກອນ

_____ 10. October

j. gɔɔ-la-gŏt
ກໍລະກົດ

_____ 11. November

k. dtu-láa
ຕຸລາ

_____ 12. December

l. míi-náa
ມີນາ

Tone Marks With High Consonants

With high consonant syllables, there are three possible tones and two tone marks which may be used.

Tone Mark	Tone Name	Tone	Examples
¯	sǐang sǎa-mán	mid	ຂາ (kaa)
̄	sǐang èek	low	ຂ່າ (kàa)

When there is no tone mark, a high consonant syllable has either rising tone or low tone depending on the combination of the vowel and the ending consonant. (See page 103-104)

Reading Exercise: <u>Read the Following Words and Practice Writing Them in Lao. Also Identify the Tones.</u>

1. ສີ່ four

2. ຫໍ່ to wrap

3. ຂ້າວ rice

4. ສົ້ນ heel

5. ຂັ້ນ step

6. ຫັ່ນ to slice

7. ຜ້າ cloth

8. ໃຫ້ to give

9. ຝິ່ນ opium

10. ຖ້ຳ cave

11. ຫ້າມ to prohibit

12. ສົ້ມ orange

13. ຫ້າ five

14. ເຝົ້າ to watch over

Read The Following Aloud

1. ຂ່າ　ຂ້າ　ຂາ　　　　6. ສື່　ສື້　ສື

2. ຖຸ່　ຖຸ້　ຖຸ　　　　7. ແພ່　ແພ້　ແພ

3. ໄຜ່　ໄຜ້　ໄຜ　　　　8. ເສົ່າ　ເສົ້າ　ເສົາ

4. ທຳ່　ທຳ້　ທຳ　　　　9. ໂຂ່　ໂຂ້　ໂຂ

5. ແຊ່　ແຊ້　ແຊ　　　10. ຕີ່　ຕີ້　ຕີ

Writing Exercise 5

Transcribe the following into Lao script.

1. sɔi _____　　　11. sǔai _____

2. pᵘ̀ng _____　　　12. fang _____

3. hᵘ̀an _____　　　13. tii _____

4. kǒm _____　　　14. faan _____

5. pɨɨn _____　　　15. kǎai _____

6. tɔɔi _____　　　16. kào _____

7. song _____　　　17. hɔ̀ng _____

8. kᵘ̀ut _____　　　18. fàai _____

9. pǝǝi _____　　　19. sàap _____

10. tǎam _____　　　20. sèn _____

Low Consonants
ອັກສອນຕ່ຳ (ǎk-sɔ̌ɔn-dtam)

There are twelve "low" consonants in Lao. You have seen five of them before as sonorant finals (ງ, ນ, ມ, ຍ, ວ) .

Consonant			Consonant Name	Sound
ຄ	ຄ	ຄວາຍ	kɔ́ɔ kwáai - buffalo	/k/
ງ	ງ	ງົວ	ngɔ́ɔ ngúa - cow	/ng/
ຊ	ຊ	ຊ້າງ	sɔ́ɔ sâang - elephant	/s/
ຍ	ຍ	ຍຸງ	nyɔ́ɔ nyúng - mosquito	/ny/
ທ	ທ	ທຸງ	tɔ́ɔ túng - flag	/t/
ນ	ນ	ນົກ	nɔ́ɔ nok - bird	/n/
ພ	ພ	ພູ	pɔ́ɔ púu - mountain	/p/
ຟ	ຟ	ໄຟ	fɔ́ɔ fái - fire	/f/
ມ	ມ	ແມວ	mɔ́ɔ mɛ́ɛo - cat	/m/
ລ	ລ	ລິງ	lɔ́ɔ líng - monkey	/l/
ວ	ວ	ວີ	wɔ́ɔ wíi - fan	/w/
ຮ	ຮ	ເຮືອນ	hɔ́ɔ hɨ́an - house	/h/

Lesson 6

'ào', 'yàak' (to want); 'gàm-láng' (to be ... ing);
tone rules for low consonants

bŏt-tíi hŏk   ບົດທິ ຫົກ   Lesson 6

kám-săp   ຄຳສັບ   Vocabulary

gàm-láng	ກຳລັງ	to be ...ing
gàm-láng ja	ກຳລັງຈະ	to be going to
bɔɔ kɔi .../bpaan-dăi	ບໍ່ຄ່ອຍ..../ ປານໃດ	not so ...
bɔɔ ... lə́əi	ບໍ່ .... ເລີຍ	not ... at all
jang-dăi/yaang-dăi	ຈັ່ງໃດ/ ຍ່າງໃດ	how
yàak	ຍາກ	to want to do something[1]
ào	ເອົາ	to want something[1]
kə́əi	ເຄີຍ	ever, used to
bpŏk-ga-dtĭ	ປົກກະຕິ	normally
bpa-jàm	ປະຈຳ	usually
lửai-lửai	ເລື້ອຍໆ	often
nyang/tửa	ຍັງ/ເທື່ອ	yet, still
yáng bɔɔ tán dâi ___ tửa		not ___ yet
ຍັງບໍ່ທັນໄດ້ ___ ເທື່ອ		
lɛ̂ɛo/lɛ̂ɛo-lɛ̂ɛo	ແລ້ວ/ແລ້ວໆ	already
dìi	ດີ	good
fáng	ຟັງ	to listen
wâo/lóm	ເວົ້າ/ລົມ	to chat, talk
pop/pɔ̂ɔ	ພົບ/ພໍ້	to meet, find
nang	ນັ່ງ	to sit
yửun	ຍືນ	to stand
nyaang	ຍ່າງ	to walk
lɛɛn	ແລ່ນ	to run
sửu	ຊື້	to buy
kăai	ຂາຍ	to sell

hɔ̂ɔng ຮ້ອງ	to sing, cry out
dtên ເຕັ້ນ	to dance
fɔ̂ɔn/dtên-lám ຟ້ອນ/ເຕັ້ນລຳ	to dance (traditional)
lìn ຫຼິ້ນ	to play
bpài-hǎa ໄປຫາ	to go to see someone
máa-hǎa ມາຫາ	to come to see someone
kǎp ຂັບ	to drive
kii ຂີ່	to ride
dtǒk/lon/lôm ຕົກ/ຫຼົ່ນ/ລົ້ມ	to fall
wîak ວຽກ	work
tu-la/wîak ຫຸລະ/ວຽກ	errand
péeng ເພງ	song
dòoi ໂດຍ	by
lot ລົດ	vehicle, car
lot-fai ລົດໄຟ	train
lot-fai-dtâi-dìn ລົດໄຟໃຕ້ດິນ	subway
lot-mée/lot-dòoi-sǎan ລົດເມ/ລົດໂດຍສານ	bus
dtak-sii/tɛk-sii ຕັກຊີ/ແທກຊີ	taxi
lot-sɔ̌ɔng-tɛ̌ɛo ລົດສອງແຖວ	minibus
lot-sǎam-lɔ̂ɔ ລົດສາມລໍ້	tricycle
lot-dtuk-dtuk ລົດຕຸກໆ	tricycle taxi
lot-jǎk ລົດຈັກ	motorcycle
lot-tìip ລົດຖີບ	bicycle
hǔa-bìn/yón ເຮືອບິນ/ຍົນ	airplane
hǔa ເຮືອ	boat, ship
fǒn ຝົນ	rain
hi-ma ຫິມະ	snow
dtôn-mâi ຕົ້ນໄມ້	tree
púu ພູ	mountain
ta-lée ທະເລ	sea

mεε-nâm   ແມ່ນ້ຳ   river

dìn   ດິນ   soil

lóm   ລົມ   wind

fái   ໄຟ   fire

hâan-lám-wóng   ຮ້ານລຳວົງ   disco

káa-láa-òo-gě   ຄາລາໂອເກະ   karaoke

kɔ̌ɔ-wâo gǎp   ຂໍເວົ້າກັບ   "May I speak with ...?"

Conversation

Somsuk: aa-lŏo. kɔ̌ɔ wâo gàp juu-ĥi dɛɛ.

ສົມສຸກ: ອາໂຫຼ.   ຂໍ ເວົ້າ ກັບ ຈູລີ່   ແດ່?

Hello! May I speak with Julie?

Julie: gàmláng wâo yuu.

ຈູລີ່:   ກຳລັງ   ເວົ້າ   ຢູ່.

Speaking.

Somsuk: jâo gàm-láng het nyǎng yuu.

ສົມສຸກ: ເຈົ້າ   ກຳລັງ   ເຮັດ   ຫຍັງ   ຢູ່?

What are you doing Julie?

Julie: kɔ̀i gàm-láng gìn kào. jâo gìn kâo lɛ̂ɛo bɔɔ.

ຈູລີ່:   ຂ້ອຍ   ກຳລັງ   ກິນ   ເຂົ້າ. ເຈົ້າ ກິນ ເຂົ້າ   ແລ້ວ ບໍ່?

I'm going to eat. Have you eaten?

Somsuk: gìn lɛ̂ɛo la.

ສົມສຸກ: ກິນ   ແລ້ວ   ລະ.

Yes, I have.

mûu-nîi kɔ̀i yàak bpài ĥin káa-láa-òo-gě.

ມື້ນີ້   ຂ້ອຍ ຢາກ ໄປ ຫຼິ້ນ   ຄາລາໂອເກະ,

I'm going to Karaoke today.

jâo ja bpai nám kɔ̀i bɔɔ.

ເຈົ້າ ຈະ ໄປ ນຳ ຂ້ອຍ ບໍ່?

Do you want to go with me today?

Julie: bpài. kɔ̀i nyáng bɔɔ tán kə́əi bpài jǎk ŧɯa.

ຈູລີ່:   ໄປ.   ຂ້ອຍ ຍັງ   ບໍ່   ທັນ ເຄີຍ ໄປ ຈັກ ເທື່ອ.

Yes. I've never been to one yet.

bpà-nyòok   ປະໂຫຍກ   **Sentences**

1. A: pûak-jâo gàm-láng het yǎng.
      ພວກເຈົ້າ   ກຳລັງ   ເຮັດ   ຫຍັງ?
      What are you doing?

   B: pûak-háo gám-láng gìn kào.
      ພວກເຮົາ   ກຳລັງ   ກິນ   ເຂົ້າ.
      We are eating.

   C: pûak-jâo gàm-láng ja het yǎng.
      ພວກເຈົ້າ   ກຳລັງ   ຈະ ເຮັດ ຫຍັງ?
      What are you going to do?

   D: pûak-háo gám-láng ja bɔng tóo-la-tat.
      ພວກເຮົາ   ກຳລັງ   ຈະ   ເບິ່ງ   ໂທລະຫັດ.
      We are going to watch T.V.

2. A: jâo gìn kào lêεo bɔɔ.
      ເຈົ້າ ກິນ ເຂົ້າ ແລ້ວ ບໍ່?
      Have you eaten?

   B: gìn lêεo.
      ກິນ   ແລ້ວ.
      Yes, I have.

   C: nyáng bɔɔ tán dâi gìn tɯa.
      ຍັງ   ບໍ່ ທັນ ໄດ້ ກິນ ເທື່ອ.
      No, I haven't.

   D: jâo bɔng tóo-la-tat lêεo bɔɔ.
      ເຈົ້າ ເບິ່ງ   ໂທລະຫັດ ແລ້ວ ບໍ່?
      Have you watched T.V.?

   E: bɔng lêεo-lêεo.
      ເບິ່ງ   ແລ້ວໆ.
      Yes, I have.

F: nyáng, nyáng bɔɔ dâi bəng tɯa.

ຍັງ,   ຍັງ   ບໍ່ ໄດ້ ເບິ່ງ ເທື່ອ.

No, I haven't.

3.   A: jâo yàak (ja) het nyǎng.

ເຈົ້າ ຢາກ (ຈະ) ເຮັດ ຫຍັງ?

What do you want to do?

B: kɔ̀i yàak (ja) gìn kào.

ຂ້ອຍ ຢາກ (ຈະ) ກິນ ເຂົ້າ.

I want to eat.

C: kɔ̀i yàak (ja) bəng tóo-la-tat.

ຂ້ອຍ ຢາກ (ຈະ) ເບິ່ງ ໂທລະທັດ.

I want to watch T.V.

4.   A: jâo kə́əi dâi bpài mɯang láao bɔɔ.

ເຈົ້າ ເຄີຍ ໄດ້ ໄປ ເມືອງ ລາວ ບໍ່?

Have you ever been to Laos?

 B: kə́əi.

ເຄີຍ.

Yes, I have.

C: bɔɔ kə́əi.

ບໍ່ ເຄີຍ

No, I haven't.

D: jâo kə́əi kii lot dtuk-dtuk lέεo bɔɔ.

ເຈົ້າ ເຄີຍ ຂີ່ ລົດ ຕຸກໆ   ແລ້ວ ບໍ່?

Have you ever ridden a tricycle taxi?

E: kə́əi kii lέεo.

ເຄີຍ ຂີ່ ແລ້ວ.

Yes, I already have.

F: nyáng, nyáng bɔɔ kə́əi kii.

ຍັງ,   ຍັງ ບໍ່ ເຄີຍ ຂີ່.

No, I haven't.

5. A: àn nîi bɔɔ kɔi dìi.

ອັນ ນີ້ ບໍ່ ຄ່ອຍ ດີ.

This one is not very good.

B: kɔi bɔɔ kɔi mak àa-hǎan fa-lang.

ຂ້ອຍ ບໍ່ ຄ່ອຍ ມັກ ອາຫານ ຝຣັ່ງ.

I don't like foreign food very much.

C: taan kámpan bɔɔ kɔi mǐi ngə́n lǎai bpàan-dǎi.

ທ່ານ ຄຳພັນ ບໍ່ ຄ່ອຍ ມີ ເງິນ ຫລາຍ ປານໃດ.

Mr. Kampan does not have very much money.

6. A: àn-nîi bɔɔ kɔi dìi bpàan-dǎi.

ອັນນີ້ ບໍ່ ຄ່ອຍ ດີ ປານໃດ.

This one is not good at all.

B: kɔi bɔɔ kɔi mak àa-hǎan fa-làng bpàan-dǎi.

ຂ້ອຍ ບໍ່ ຄ່ອຍ ມັກ ອາຫານ ຝຣັ່ງ ປານໃດ.

I don't like western food at all.

C: taan kámpan bɔɔ mǐi ngə́n jǎk-nɔi lə́əi.

ທ່ານ ຄຳພັນ ບໍ່ ມີ ເງິນ ຈັກໜ້ອຍ ເລີຍ.

Mr. Kampan does not have any money at all.

7. A: taan kámpan bpài gìn àa-hǎan láao bpa-jàm.

ທ່ານ ຄຳພັນ ໄປ ກິນ ອາຫານ ລາວ ປະຈຳ.

Mr. Kampan goes to eat Lao food regularly.

B: taan kámpan bpài gìn àa-hǎan láao lûai lûai.

ທ່ານ ຄຳພັນ ໄປ ກິນ ອາຫານ ລາວ ເລື້ອຍໆ.

Mr. Kampan goes to eat Laos food often.

C: taan kámpan bpài gìn àa-hǎan láao tuk wán-put.

ທ່ານ ຄຳພັນ ໄປ ກິນ ອາຫານ ລາວ ທຸກ ວັນພຸດ.

Mr. Kampan goes to eat Lao food every Wednesday.

8. A: bpǒk-ga-dǐ jâo bpài het wîak jang dǎi.

ປົກກະຕິ ເຈົ້າ ໄປ ເຮັດ ວຽກ ຈັ່ງ ໃດ?

How do you normally go to work?

B: kǎp lot bpài.

ຂັບ   ລົດ   ໄປ.

I drive.

C: nang dtak-sii bpài.

ນັ່ງ   ຕັກຊີ   ໄປ.

I take a taxi.

D: kii lot jǎk bpài.

ຂີ່   ລົດ   ຈັກ   ໄປ.

I ride a motorcycle.

E: nyaang bpài.

ຍ່າງ   ໄປ.

I walk.

9. A: jâo bpài sǎi máa.

ເຈົ້າ   ໄປ   ໃສ   ມາ?

Where have you been?

B: kɔ̀i bpài gìn kào máa.

ຂ້ອຍ ໄປ   ກິນ   ເຂົ້າ   ມາ.

I went to eat.

C: jâo sɨ̀ɨ nyǎng (máa).

ເຈົ້າ   ຊື້   ຫຍັງ   (ມາ) ?

What did you buy?

D: kɔ̀i sɨ̀ɨ kà-nǒm (máa).

ຂ້ອຍ   ຊື້   ຂະໜົມ   (ມາ) .

I bought snacks.

máa (ມາ) at the end of these sentences literally means to have
done something and come back, which implies the past tense.

10. A: kɔ̀i yàak bpài hǎa jâo.

ຂ້ອຍ   ຢາກ   ໄປ   ຫາ   ເຈົ້າ.

I want to go to see you.

B: mûu-wáan-nîi láao máa hăa kɔ̀i.

ມື້ ວານ ນີ້ ລາວ ມາ ຫາ ຂ້ອຍ.

Yesterday he came to see me.

C: láao tóo-la-săp máa-hăa jâo.

ລາວ ໂທລະສັບ ມາຫາ ເຈົ້າ.

He gave you a call.

D: kɔ̀i nyaang bpài-hăa láao.

ຂ້ອຍ ຍ່າງ ໄປຫາ ລາວ.

I walk to (meet) him.

11.   fŏn gàm-láng dtŏk.

ຝົນ ກຳລັງ ຕົກ.

It's raining.

12.   kɔ̀i kii lot bpài het wîak.

ຂ້ອຍ ຂີ່ ລົດ ໄປ ເຮັດ ວຽກ.

I go to work by car.

13.   kɔ̀i mak lóm nám kón láao.

ຂ້ອຍ ມັກ ລົມ ນຳ ຄົນ ລາວ.

We like to talk to Lao people.

14.   yuu mûang láao bɔɔ mîi hi-ma.

ຢູ່ ເມືອງ ລາວ ບໍ່ ມີ ຫິມະ.

There is no snow in Laos.

15.   yuu tɔng púu bɔɔ kɔi mîi dtôn-mâi.

ຢູ່ ເທິງ ພູ ບໍ່ ຄ່ອຍ ມີ ຕົ້ນໄມ້.

There are not so many trees in the mountains.

16.   bɔɔ mîi kón yuu hûan lɔ́əi.

ບໍ່ ມີ ຄົນ ຢູ່ ເຮືອນ ເລີຍ.

There isn't anybody at home at all.

17.   mûu-nîi kɔ̀i mîi wîak lăai, kɔ̀i bpài-hăa jâo bɔɔ dâi dɔ̀ɔk.

ມື້ນີ້ ຂ້ອຍ ມີ ວຽກ ຫລາຍ. ຂ້ອຍ ໄປຫາ ເຈົ້າ ບໍ່ ໄດ້ ດອກ.

Today, I have a lot of errands. I can't go to see you.

18. kɔ̀i gìn kào lɛ̂ɛo.

ຂ້ອຍ ກິນ ເຂົ້າ ແລ້ວ.

I already ate.

19. kɔ̀i nyáng bɔɔ dâi gìn kào tɯa.

ຂ້ອຍ ຍັງ ບໍ່ ໄດ້ ກິນ ເຂົ້າ ເທື່ອ.

I haven't eaten yet.

20. pûak-háo fáng péeng.

ພວກເຮົາ ຟັງ ເພງ.

We listened to music.

21. láao lóm găp jâo.

ລາວ ລົມ ກັບ ເຈົ້າ.

He talked to you.

22. kɔ̀i mak aan năng-sɯ̆ɯ yuu hɯan.

ຂ້ອຍ ມັກ ອ່ານ ໜັງສື ຢູ່ ເຮືອນ.

I like to read at home.

23. mɯ̂ɯ ɯɯn kɔ̀i yàak bpài tiao găp puu-săao kɔ̆ɔng kɔ̀i.

ມື້ ອື່ນ ຂ້ອຍ ຢາກ ໄປ ທ່ຽວ ກັບ ຜູ້ສາວ ຂອງ ຂ້ອຍ.

Tomorrow I want to go out with my girlfriend.

24. dtɔ̀ɔn-nîi láao nyáng bɔɔ yàak hían páa-săa-láao tɯa.

ຕອນນີ້ ລາວ ຍັງ ບໍ່ ຢາກ ຮຽນ ພາສາລາວ ເທື່ອ.

He doesn't want to study Lao at the moment.

25. mɯ̂ɯ-nîi kɔ̀i bɔɔ yàak het nyăng.

ມື້ນີ້ ຂ້ອຍ ບໍ່ ຢາກ ເຮັດ ຫຍັງ.

Today I don't want to do anything.

Test 6

Match the English verbs with the Lao verbs.

_____	1. to talk/chat	a. fǎng	ຟັງ
_____	2. to listen	b. lɛɛn	ແລ່ນ
_____	3. to take a trip	c. dtǒk	ຕົກ
_____	4. to play	d. hɔ̂ɔng	ຮ້ອງ
_____	5. to wake up	e. nyaang	ຍ່າງ
_____	6. to drive	f. lɛ̂ɛo	ແລ້ວ
_____	7. to sit	g. y<u>ùu</u>n	ຢືນ
_____	8. to run	h. bpài-tiao	ໄປທ່ຽວ
_____	9. to walk	i. lîn	ຫລິ້ນ
_____	10. to buy	j. aan	ອ່ານ
_____	11. to sell	k. s<u>ûu</u>	ຊື້
_____	12. to sing	l. dt<u>ùu</u>n	ຕື່ນ
_____	13. to fall	m. yàak	ຢາກ
_____	14. to want to	n. nang	ນັ່ງ
_____	15. to stand	o. lóm	ລົ້ມ
		p. kǎp	ຂັບ
		q. kǎai	ຂາຍ

Translate the following into English.

1. dtɔ̀ɔn-nîi kɔ̀i gàm-láng ja bpài dən-bìn.
    ຕອນນີ້   ຂ້ອຍ   ກຳລັງ   ຈະ   ໄປ   ເດີ່ນບິນ.

    _____

2. bpǒk-ga-dtǐ taan kám-pán kii lot-fái bpài het wîak.
    ປົກກະຕິ   ທ່ານ   ຄຳພັນ   ຂີ່   ລົດໄຟ   ໄປ   ເຮັດ   ວຽກ.

    _____

3. pûak-háo yàak míi hâan-àa-hǎan láao yuu àa-mée-li-gàa.
    ພວກ–ເຮົາ   ຢາກ   ມີ   ຮ້ານອາຫານ   ລາວ   ຢູ່   ອາເມລິກາ.

    _____

4. láao yuu mɨ́ang tái dtâng-dtɛɛ dɨ̀an mi-tu-náa.
    ລາວ   ຢູ່   ເມືອງ   ໄຫ   ຕັ້ງແຕ່   ເດືອນ   ມິຖຸນາ.

    _____

5. kɔ̀i bɔɔ mak fáng péeng.
    ຂ້ອຍ   ບໍ່   ມັກ   ຟັງ   ເພງ.

    _____

Practice Writing the Low Consonants

There are 12 "low" consonants in Lao. We have already practiced five letters in the final consonants section in Lesson 3. Here are all of them again. Start near the ❶.

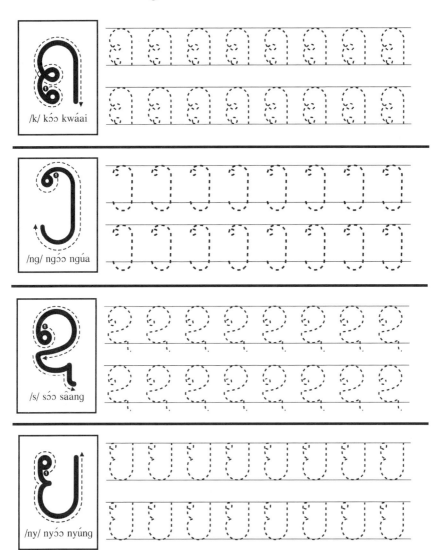

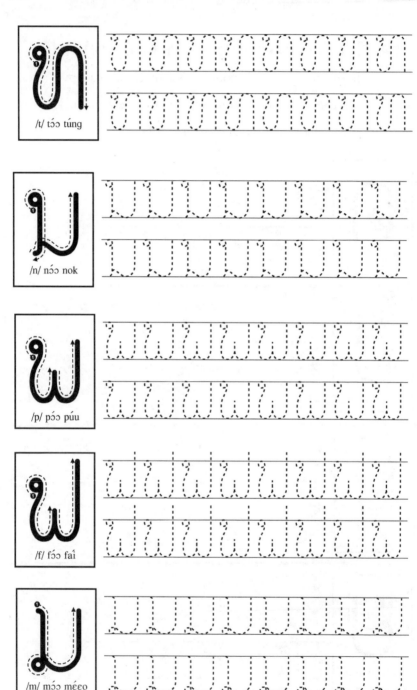

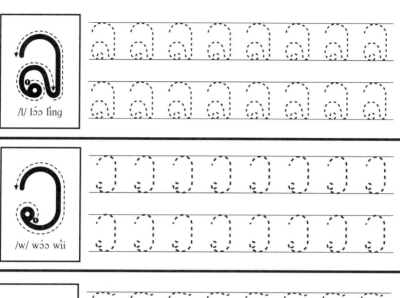

/l/ lɔ́ɔ líng

 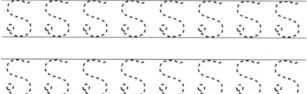

/w/ wɔ́ɔ wíi

/h/ hɔ́ɔ hŭan

Tone Rules for Low Consonants

In the absence of a tone mark, the tone rules for low consonants are as follows:

Low Consonant with Live Syllable = High Tone

Low Consonant with Short Vowel and Dead Syllable = Mid Tone

Low Consonant with Long Vowel and Dead Syllable = Falling Tone

Notice that there are two kinds of dead syllables with the low consonants. The first kind has a short vowel either in final position or followed by a stop final. The second kind has a long vowel followed by a stop final.

Examples:

Low Consonant + Long Vowel = High Tone

		Sound Produced	Meaning
ม + –า		= มา (máa)	come
ฟ + ไ–		= ไฟ (fái)	fire
ม + ◌ื		= มื (múu)	hand

Exercise: <u>Read the Following Words and Practice Writing Them</u>
<u>in Lao.</u>

1.   ເມຍ wife   2.   ວີ fan

3.   ພໍ enough   4.   ໄຟ fire

5.   ລາ to say good-bye 6.   ທີ time

7.   ເຮືອ ship   8.   ນາຍ boss

9.   ເມົາ drunk   10.   ງາ sesame

11.   ໃນ in   12.   ພາ to take

13.   ເຮົາ we   14.   ເນີຍ cheese

Writing Exercise 6

Transcribe the following into Lao script.

1. páa _____

2. sóo _____

3. hám _____

4. móo _____

5. sĭa _____

6. lía _____

7. sə́əi _____

8. túa _____

9. hŭa _____

10. fáo _____

11. tíi _____

12. yɔ́ɔ _____

13. fúu _____

14. tée _____

15. kɔ́ɔ _____

16. kɨ́ɨ _____

17. ngáa _____

18. pέε _____

19. yám _____

20. lə́əi _____

Lesson 7

'dâi-yín' (to hear); 'jɨɨ' (to remember);
'nɔ́ɔn-lǎp' (to fall asleep); 'bəng' (to look);
tone rules for low consonants (cont.)

bŏt-tíi jĕt ບົດທິ ເຈັດ Lesson 7

kám-săp ຄຳສັບ Vocabulary

pǎi ໃຜ		who
kɔ̌ɔng ຂອງ		of
kɔ̌ɔng pǎi ຂອງໃຜ		whose
dâi ໄດ້		can
bɔɔ dâi ບໍ່ໄດ້ (after a verb)		cannot
bɔɔ dâi ບໍ່ໄດ້ (before a verb)		did not
lɔ́ɔi-nâam ລອຍນ້ຳ		to swim
jɯɯ/jàm ຈື່		to memorize
jɯɯ dâi ຈື່ໄດ້		to remember
jɯɯ bɔɔ dâi ຈື່ບໍ່ໄດ້		can't remember
(jâo) jɯɯ dâi bɔɔ (ເຈົ້າ) ຈື່ໄດ້ບໍ?		Do you remember?
yín/dâi-yín/hûu-yín ຍິນ/ໄດ້ຍິນ/ຮູ້ຍິນ		to hear, can hear
bɔɔ dâi-yín ບໍ່ໄດ້ຍິນ		can't hear
(jâo) dâi-yín bɔɔ (ເຈົ້າ) ໄດ້ຍິນບໍ່		Can you hear?
bəng ເບິ່ງ		to look
hěn/bəng-hěn ເຫັນ/ເບິ່ງເຫັນ		to see, can see
(bəng) bɔɔ hěn (ເບິ່ງ) ບໍ່ເຫັນ		can't see
jâo (bəng) hěn bɔɔ ເຈົ້າ(ເບິ່ງ) ເຫັນບໍ?		Can you see?
hûu/sâap/hûu-jăk ຮູ້/ຊາບ/ຮູ້ຈັກ		to know[1]
nɔ́ɔn-lăp ນອນຫລັບ		to fall asleep
nɔ́ɔn bɔɔ lăp ນອນບໍ່ຫລັບ		can't fall asleep
lέεo/săm-lĕt ແລ້ວ/ສຳເລັດ		to finish
ngǎo-nɔ́ɔn ເຫງົານອນ		sleepy
dàng/sǐang-dàng ດັງ/ສຽງດັງ		loud

nùak-hǔu ໜວກຫູ	bothered by loud noise
(ǐt) mɯai (ອິດ) ເມື່ອຍ	tired
tán (wée-láa) ທັນ (ເວລາ)	on time, to keep up with
ɔ̀ɔk ອອກ	out
kit ຄິດ	to think
kit-hɔ̂ɔt ຄິດຮອດ	to think about, miss
kit waa ຄິດວ່າ	to think that ...
nyáam-dǎi/mɯa-dǎi ຍາມໃດ/ເມື່ອໃດ	When?
sâa/sâa-sâa ຊ້າ/ຊ້າໆ	slow/slowly
wái/wái-wái ໄວ/ໄວໆ	quick/quickly
tɯ̀ɯk ຖືກ	correct
pǐt ຜິດ	incorrect
tɛ̂ɛ/jìng/ii-lǐi ແທ້/ຈິງ/ອີ່ຫລີ	true, really
sɛ̂ɛp ແຊບ	delicious
wǎan ຫວານ	sweet
kém ເຄັມ	salty
jɯ̀ɯt ຈືດ	tasteless
sòm ສົ້ມ	sour
pět ເຜັດ	spicy, hot

1. sâap -"to know" is a polite form of hûu . Both sâap and
   húu are used without an object. hûu-jǎk can be used
   with or without an object.
   e.g. kɔ̀i bɔɔ hûu. or kɔ̀i bɔɔ sâap. = I don't know
        kɔ̀i bɔɔ hûu-jàk láao. = I don't know him.

Conversation

Jane: sɔ̌ɔn, hɯ́an jâo yuu-sai .

ເຈນ: ສອນ, ເຮືອນ ເຈົ້າ ຢູ່ໃສ?

    Where is your house, Sorn?

Son: yuu lǔang-pa-bàang. jâo hûu bɔɔ waa mán yuu sǎi.

ສອນ: ຢູ່ ຫລວງພະບາງ. ເຈົ້າ ຮູ້ ບໍ່ ວ່າ ມັນ ຢູ່ ໃສ?

    In Luang Phrabang. Do you know where that is?

Jane: hûu. kɔ̀i hûu-jǎk

ເຈນ: ຮູ້. ຂ້ອຍ ຮູ້ຈັກ.

    Yes, I do.

Son: jâo máa mɯ́ang láao dâi jǎk bpìi lέεo.

ສອນ: ເຈົ້າ ມາ ເມືອງ ລາວ ໄດ້ ຈັກ ປີ ແລ້ວ?

    When did you come to Laos?

Jane: bpa-máan sǎam bpìi lêεo.

ເຈນ: ປະມານ ສາມ ປີ ແລ້ວ.

    About three years ago.

Son: jâo mak àa-hǎan láao bɔɔ.

ສອນ: ເຈົ້າ ມັກ ອາຫານ ລາວ ບໍ່?

    Do you like Lao food?

Jane: mak. àa-hǎan láao sêεp lǎai. kɔ̀i mak gìn pět.

ເຈນ: ມັກ. ອາຫານ ລາວ ແຊບ ຫລາຍ. ຂ້ອຍ ມັກ ກິນ ເຜັດ.

    Yes. Lao food is very good. I like spicy food.

Son: jâo aan páa-sǎa láao dâi bɔɔ.

ສອນ: ເຈົ້າ ອ່ານ ພາສາ ລາວ ໄດ້ ບໍ່?

    Can you read Lao?

Jane: aan dâi nɔ̀i nɯng. dtεε kǐan bɔɔ dâi.

ເຈນ: ອ່ານ ໄດ້ ໜ້ອຍ ນຶ່ງ. ແຕ່ ຂຽນ ບໍ່ ໄດ້.

    I can read a little, but I can't write.

Son: jâo fáng tán bɔɔ.

ສອນ: ເຈົ້າ ຟັງ ທັນ ບໍ່?

      Can you understand (spoken Lao)?

      (Literally: Can you catch up with listening?)

Jane: tàa wâo sâa-sâa, gɔɔ fáng tán yuu.

ເຈນ: ຖ້າ ເວົ້າ ຊ້າໆ, ກໍ ຟັງ ທັນ ຢູ່.

      If (you) speak slowly, I can understand.

      tàa wâo wái lăai, gɔɔ fáng bɔɔ kɔi tán.

      ຖ້າ ເວົ້າ ໄວ ຫລາຍ ກໍ ຟັງ ບໍ່ ຄ່ອຍ ທັນ.

      If (you) speak fast, I don't understand very well.

bpà-nyòok   ປະໂຫຍກ   Sentences

1. A: nîi mɛn păi.
     ນີ້ ແມ່ນ ໃຜ?
     Who is this?

   B: nîi mɛn kám-pán.
     ນີ້ ແມ່ນ ຄຳພັນ.
     This is Mr. Kampan.

2. A: nîi kɔ̌ɔng păi.
     ນີ້ ຂອງ ໃຜ?
     Whose is this?

   B: nîi kɔ̌ɔng kɔi.
     ນີ້ ຂອງ ຂ້ອຍ.
     This is mine.

   A: nîi hŭan (kɔ̌ɔng)* păi.
     ນີ້ ເຮືອນ (ຂອງ) ໃຜ?
     Whose house is this?

   B: nîi hŭan (kɔ̌ɔng) kɔi.
     ນີ້ ເຮືອນ (ຂອງ) ຂ້ອຍ.
     This is my house.

   * kɔ̌ɔng can be omitted when used with noun.

3. A: jâo lɔ́ɔi-nâam bpèn bɔɔ.
       ເຈົ້າ   ລອຍນ້ຳ   ເປັນ   ບໍ່?
       Can you swim?

    B: lɔ́ɔi bpèn yuu.
       ລອຍ ເປັນ   ຢູ່.
       Yes, I can.

    C: lɔ́ɔi bɔɔ bpèn.
       ລອຍ ບໍ່   ເປັນ.
       No, I can't.

4. A: jɯɯ kɔ̀i dâi bɔɔ.
       ຈື່   ຂ້ອຍ ໄດ້   ບໍ່?
       Do you remember me?

    B: jɯɯ dâi yuu.
       ຈື່   ໄດ້   ຢູ່.
       Yes, I do.

    C: jɯɯ bɔɔ dâi.
       ຈື່   ບໍ່   ໄດ້.
       No, I don't.

5. A: dâi-yín bɔɔ.
       ໄດ້ຍິນ   ບໍ່?
       Can you hear?

    B: dâi-yín.
       ໄດ້ຍິນ.
       Yes, I can.

    C: bɔɔ dâi-yín.
       ບໍ່   ໄດ້ຍິນ.
       No, I can't.

6. A: hěn láao bɔɔ.
       ເຫັນ ລາວ ບໍ່?
       Can you see him?

    B: hěn.
        ເຫັນ.
        Yes, I can.

C: bɔɔ hěn.

ບໍ່ ເຫັນ.

No, I can't.

7. A: hûu-jǎk láao bɔɔ.

ຮູ້ຈັກ ລາວ ບໍ?

Do you know him?

B: hûu-jǎk.

ຮູ້ຈັກ

Yes, I do.

C: bɔɔ, bɔɔ hûu-jǎk.

ບໍ່, ບໍ່ ຮູ້ຈັກ.

No, I don't.

8. A: lêɛo lêɛo bɔɔ.*

ແລ້ວ ແລ້ວ ບໍ?

Are you ready?/Have you finished?

B: lêɛo lêɛo.*

ແລ້ວ ແລ້ວ.

Yes, I am./Yes, I have.

* The first lêɛo means "to finish" or to "to get done" and the second
  one means "already".

C: nyáng bɔɔ lêɛo.

ຍັງ ບໍ່ ແລ້ວ.

No, I'm not./No, I haven't.

9.   mûa-kúun-nîi kɔ̀i nɔ́ɔn bɔɔ kɔi lǎp.

ມື້ ຄືນ ນີ້ ຂ້ອຍ ນອນ ບໍ່ ຄ່ອຍ ຫລັບ.

I didn't sleep very well last night.

10.   mûa-kúun-nîi kɔ̀i nɔ́ɔn lǎp dìi.

ມື້ ຄືນ ນີ້ ຂ້ອຍ ນອນ ຫລັບ ດີ.

I slept very well last night.

11. A: kɔ̀i ngǎo-nɔ́ɔn lǎai.

ຂ້ອຍ ເຫງົາ-ນອນ ຫລາຍ.

I'm really sleepy.

B: kɔi mɯai têɛ-têɛ.

ຂ້ອຍ ເມື່ອຍ ແທ້ໆ.

I'm really tired.

C: nùak-hǔu têɛ-têɛ.

ໜວກຫູ ແທ້ໆ.

It's really noisy.

D: dìi kak têɛ-têɛ .

ດິ ຄັກ ແທ້ໆ .

It's really good.

12.   sǐang dàng lǎai.

ສຽງ ດັງ ຫລາຍ.

The noise is very loud.

13.   láao fáng páa-sǎa láao bɔɔ tán.

ລາວ ຟັງ ພາສາ ລາວ ບໍ່ ທັນ.

He can't understand spoken Lao.

(Literally: He can't keep up with listening to the Lao language.)

14.   kɔi aan ngǎng-sɯɯ láao bɔɔ ɔɔk.*

ຂ້ອຍ ອ່ານ ໜັງສື ລາວ ບໍ່ ອອກ.

I can't read Lao.

15.   kɔi gìn pět bɔɔ dâi.

ຂ້ອຍ ກິນ ແຜັດ ບໍ່ ໄດ້.

I can't eat hot food.

16.   kɔi bɔɔ gìn pět.

ຂ້ອຍ ບໍ່ ກິນ ແຜັດ.

I didn't eat hot food.

---

* ɔɔk is often used with the verbs, fáng, aan, kǐan.

  e.g. fáng bɔɔ ɔɔk. or fang bɔɔ dâi.

  = I don't/can't understand. or I can't get what is being said.

17. kɔ̀i bpài mɨang-láao bɔɔ dâi.
    ຂ້ອຍ ໄປ ເມືອງລາວ ບໍ່ ໄດ້.
    I can't go to Laos.

18. kɔ̀i bɔɔ dâi bpài mɨang láao.
    ຂ້ອຍ ບໍ່ ໄດ້ ໄປ ເມືອງ ລາວ.
    I didn't go to Laos.

19. kɔ̀i kit-hɔ̀ɔt jâo lǎai.
    ຂ້ອຍ ຄິດຮອດ ເຈົ້າ ຫລາຍ.
    I miss you very much.

20. pûak-háo gàm-láng bəng ta-lée.
    ພວກເຮົາ ກຳລັງ ເບິ່ງ ທະເລ.
    We are looking at the sea.

21. kɔ̀i wâo páa-sǎa-láao bɔɔ kɔi tɨ̀ɨk.
    ຂ້ອຍ ເວົ້າ ພາສາລາວ ບໍ່ ຄ່ອຍ ຖືກ.
    I don't speak Lao very correctly.

22. láao aan páa-sǎa àng-gǐt dâi yaang bɔɔ pìt jǎk-dtoo lə̂əi.
    ລາວ ອ່ານ ພາສາ ອັງກິດ ໄດ້ ຢ່າງ ບໍ່ ຜິດ ຈັກໂຕ ເລີຍ.
    He reads English without making mistakes at all.
    (Literally: He reads English not incorrectly at all.)

23. A: kɔ̀i (kit) waa mán sɛ̂ɛp.
    ຂ້ອຍ (ຄິດ) ວ່າ ມັນ ແຊບ.
    I think it's delicious.

   B: kɔ̀i kit waa àa-hǎan láao sɛ̂ɛp lǎai.
    ຂ້ອຍ ຄິດ ວ່າ ອາຫານ ລາວ ແຊບ ຫລາຍ.
    I think Lao food is very delicious.

   C: kɔ̀i kit waa àa-hǎan láao sɛ̂ɛp ii-lǐi.
    ຂ້ອຍ ຄິດ ວ່າ ອາຫານ ລາວ ແຊບ ອີ່ຫລີ.
    I think Lao food is really delicious.

   D: kɔ̀i kit waa mán pět.
    ຂ້ອຍ ຄິດ ວ່າ ມັນ ເຜັດ.
    I think it's spicy.

E: kɔ̀i kit waa àa-hǎan láao pĕt.

ຂ້ອຍ ຄິດ ວ່າ   ອາຫານ   ລາວ   ເຜັດ.

I think Lao food is spicy.

F: kɔ̀i kit waa àa-hǎan láao pĕt ii-lǐi.

ຂ້ອຍ ຄິດ ວ່າ   ອາຫານ   ລາວ   ເຜັດ ອີ່ຫລີ.

I think Lao food is really spicy.

24. A: jâo kit waa ja bpài mɨ́ang láao mɨa-dǎi.

ເຈົ້າ ຄິດ ວ່າ   ຈະ ໄປ   ເມືອງ   ລາວ   ເມື່ອໃດ?

When do you think you will go to Laos?

B: kɔ̀i kit waa ja bpài dɨ̀an nàa.

ຂ້ອຍ ຄິດ ວ່າ ຈະ ໄປ   ເດືອນ ໜ້າ.

I think I will go next month.

25. A: láao sɨɨ nyǎng.

ລາວ   ຊື່ ຫຍັງ?

What's his name?

B: bɔɔ hûu. kɔ̀i kit bɔɔ ɔ̀ɔk.

ບໍ່ ຮູ້. ຂ້ອຍ ຄິດ ບໍ່ ອອກ.

I don't know. I can't think of it.

(Literally: I can't think it out.)

Test 7

Match the English words with the Lao words.

_____	1. tired	a. pǐt ຜິດ
_____	2. sleepy	b. ii-lǐi/kak ອິ່ຫລີ/ຄັກ
_____	3. to think about	c. som ສົ້ມ
_____	4. to hear	d. kit-hɔ̂ɔt ຄິດຮອດ
_____	5. sweet	e. dàng ດັງ
_____	6. salty	f. sɛ̂ɛp ແຊບ
_____	7. incorrect	g. pět ເຜັດ
_____	8. to remember	h. ngǎo-nɔ́ɔn ເຫງົ້ານອນ
_____	9. to finish	i. tùuk ຖືກ
_____	10. delicious	j. wǎan ຫວານ
_____	11. sour	k. lɛ̂ɛo ແລ້ວ
_____	12. who	l. kit ຄິດ
_____	13. loud	m. mɯai ເມື່ອຍ
_____	14. really	n. kém ເຄັມ
_____	15. correct	o. jɯɯ-dâi ຈຳໄດ້
		p. dâi-yín ໄດ້ຍິນ
		q. pǎi ໃຜ

Translate the following into English.

1. bpûm-kǐan kɔ̌ɔng pǎi yuu tǎng dto.

ປຶ້ມຮຽນ ຂອງ ໃຜ ຢູ່ ເທິງ ໂຕະ.

---

2. kɔ̀i lɔ́ɔi-nâam bɔɔ bpèn.

ຂ້ອຍ ລອຍນ້ຳ ບໍ່ ເປັນ.

---

3. kɔ̀i bɔɔ dâi lɔ́ɔi-nâam..

ຂ້ອຍ ບໍ່ ໄດ້ ລອຍນ້ຳ.

---

4. kɔ̀i kit hɔ̂ɔt mʉ́ang láao lǎai ii-lǐi.

ຂ້ອຍ ຄິດ ຮອດ ເມືອງ ລາວ ຫລາຍ ອິຫລີ.

---

5. kɔ̀i kit waa àa hǎan fa-lang bɔɔ kɔi sɛ̂ɛp.

ຂ້ອຍ ຄິດ ວ່າ ອາຫານ ຝຣັ່ງ ບໍ່ ຄ່ອຍ ແຊບ.

Tone Rules for Low Consonants (cont.)

In the absence of a tone mark, the tone rules for low consonants are as follows:

Low Consonant with Live Syllable = High Tone

Low Consonant with Long Vowel and Dead Syllable = Falling Tone

Low Consonant with Short Vowel and Dead Syllable = Mid Tone

Examples:

Low Consonant + Short Vowel = Mid Tone

	Sound Produced	Meaning
ພ + ◌ະ	= ພະ (pa)	monk
ລ + ເ◌ະ	= ເລະ (le)	mushy

Exercise: Read the Following Words and Practice Writing Them in Lao.

1.	ເຄາະ to knock	2.	ລະ to omit, per
3.	ເງາະ rambutan	4.	ແລະ and
4.	ແວະ to stop over	5.	ຫຼະ errand

Low Consonant + Any Vowel + Sonorant Final

    = High Tone

	Sound Produced	Meaning
ລ + ◌̌ + ງ	= ລີ̄ງ (líng)	monkey
ມ + ◌̌ + ນ	= ມັ̌ນ (mán)	it, potato
ຊ + −າ + ຍ	= ຊາຍ (sáai)	sand

Low Consonant + Long Vowel + Stop Final

    = Falling Tone

	Sound Produced	Meaning
ຄ + −າ + ບ	= ຄາບ (kâap)	to hold something between the teeth
ລ + ◌ຸ + ກ	= ລູ̂ກ (lûuk)	child
ມ + ◌̂ + ດ	= ມີ̂ດ (mîit)	knife

Low Consonant + Short Vowel + Stop Final

    = Mid Tone

	Sound Produced	Meaning
ຄ + ◌̌ + ບ	= ຄັບ (kap)	tight
ລ + ◌ຸ + ກ	= ລຸກ (luk)	to rise
ມ + ◌̄ + ດ	= ມິດ (mit)	entirely

Exercise: Read the Following Words and Practice Writing Them
in Lao. Also Identify the Tones.

1. ລຸງ uncle   2. ມືດ dark

3. ເລກ math   4. ທານ alms

5. ທັບ to put on top   6. ນັດ appointment

7. ຣາດ to pour over   8. ຟາງ hay

9. ວັນ day   10. ລົບ to subtract

11. ຮັບ to receive   12. ຍຸງ mosquito

13. ໂລກ earth   14. ຊຸດ set

15. ນວດ to massage   16. ນາຍ boss

17. ພັງ to collapse   18. ທາກ snail

19. ຮັກ to love   20. ທຽມ fake

Tone Marks With Low Consonants

With low consonant syllables, there are three possible tones and two tone marks which may be used.

Tone Mark	Tone Name	Tone	Examples
—	sǐang sǎa-mán	mid	ຄາ (kaa)
—	sǐang tóo	falling	ຄ້າ (kâa)

The third possible tone, high tone, occurs with live syllables and no tone marks. (Review "Tone Rules for Low Consonants" on page 158.)

Exercise: Read the Following Words and Practice Writing Them in Lao. Also Identify the Tones.

1. ມວງ purple

2. ນັ້ນ that

3. ອື້ນ piece

4. ຊັ້ນ grade, floor

5. ຟ້າ sky

6. ຄ້າງ to owe

7. ລົ້ນ to overflow

8. ມ້າ horse

9. ນີ້ this

10. ພີ່ term of endearment for an older person

Read The Following Aloud

1. ຄາ   ຄ່າ   ຄ້າ

2. ຊຸ   ຊຸ່   ຊຸ້

3. ຊຸ   ຊຸ່   ຊຸ້

4. ເຫ   ເຫ່   ເຫ້

5. ໄຟ   ໄຟ່   ໄຟ້

6. ເບົາ   ເບົ່າ   ເບົ້າ

7. ຟໍ   ຟໍ່   ຟໍ້

8. ໂມ   ໂມ່   ໂມ້

9. ແຍ   ແຍ່   ແຍ້

10. ຊີ   ຊີ່   ຊີ້

11. ເລຍ   ເລ່ຍ   ເລ້ຍ

12. ໂວ   ໂວ່   ໂວ້

Writing Exercise 7

Transcribe the following into Lao script.

1. mûang _____

2. nok _____

3. kam _____

4. nyúung _____

5. fíim _____

6. nîu _____

7. mîit _____

8. sɔ́ɔng _____

9. fáng _____

10. wɛ́ɛo _____

11. sáam _____

12. hîap _____

13. púum _____

14. hâan _____

15. hâap _____

16. wâang _____

17. nyɨ̂ang _____

18. sɛng _____

19. kok _____

20. pɨ̂a _____

Lesson 8

body parts; everyday life; Silent ฅ

bŏt-tíi bpὲεt   ບົດທິ ແປດ   **Lesson 8**
kám-săp   ຄຳສັບ   **Vocabulary**

dtàa	ຕາ	eye
hŭu	ຫູ	ear
dàng	ດັງ	nose
bpàak	ປາກ	mouth
kὲo	ແຂ້ວ	tooth
lín	ລີ້ນ	tongue
nùat	ໜວດ	mustache
káo	ເຄົາ	beard
gὲεm-bɔng	ແກ້ມບ່ອງ	dimple
kîu	ຄິ້ວ	eyebrow
pŏm	ຜົມ	hair (on the head only)
kŏn	ຂົນ	hair
kŏn-dtàa	ຂົນຕາ	eyelash
hŭa	ຫົວ	head
nàa	ໜ້າ	face
nàa-pàak	ໜ້າຜາກ	forehead
lăng	ຫລັງ	back
kɔɔ	ຄໍ	neck
tɔ̂ɔng	ທ້ອງ	stomach
săai bùu	ສາຍບື	navel
hŭa-jài	ຫົວໃຈ	heart
nóm	ນົມ	breast
ɔ̆k	ເອິກ	chest
mùu	ມື	hand
nîu/nîu-mùu	ນີ້ວ/ ນີ້ວມື	finger
lep-mùu	ເລັບມື	nail

kɛ̌ɛn ແຂນ	arm
kǎa ຂາ	leg
hǔa-kao ຫົວເຂົ່າ	knee
dtìin ຕີນ	foot
nîu-dtìin ນີ້ວຕີນ	toe
fǎi/bpàan ໄຝ/ປານ	mole
sǐu ສິວ	pimple
nâam-dtàa ນ້ຳຕາ	tear
sa-mɔ̌ɔng ສະໝອງ	brain
dtǎp ຕັບ	liver
màak-kai-lǎng ໝາກໄຂ່ຫລັງ	kidney
sài ໃສ້	intestine
tɔ̂ɔng-nɔ̂ɔi ທ້ອງນ້ອຍ	fat stomach, paunch
ga-dùuk ກະດູກ	bone
haang-gàai ຮ່າງກາຍ	body
kɔ̌ɔng ຂອງ	thing
sɰ́ɰ-kɰang ຊື້ເຄື່ອງ	to shop, to buy things
bpài sɰ́ɰ-kɰang ໄປຊື້ເຄື່ອງ	to go shopping
sai/nung ໃສ່/ນຸ່ງ	to wear, put on
tɔ̌ɔt/bpǒt ຖອດ/ປົດ	to take off
dtɛng-dtùa ແຕ່ງຕົວ	to get dressed
bpùat ປວດ	to ache[2]
jěp ເຈັບ	to hurt[2]
bpèn-wǎt ເປັນຫວັດ	to catch a cold
dtǎt ຕັດ	to cut
tɛ̌ɛ ແຖ	to shave
lâang ລ້າງ	to wash
sǎ-pǒm ສະຜົມ	to wash hair
àap-nâm ອາບນ້ຳ	to take a bath/ shower
sak-kɰang-nung ຊັກເຄື່ອງນຸ່ງ	to do the laundry

tǔu kèo	ຖູແຂ້ວ	to brush one's teeth
bpɛ̀ɛng-tǔu-kèo	ແປງຖູແຂ້ວ	toothbrush
yàa-tǔu-kèo	ຍາຖູແຂ້ວ	toothpaste
sa-bùu	ສະບູ	soap
fɛɛp	ແຟບ	detergent
mùak	ໝວກ	hat
sừa	ເສື້ອ	shirt, blouse
sừa-yừut	ເສື້ອຍືດ	T-shirt
sừa-nyai	ເສື້ອໃຫຍ່	business suit
sừa-kɛ̌ɛn-nyáao	ເສື້ອແຂນຍາວ	long-sleeved shirt
sừa-kɛ̌ɛn-sàn	ເສື້ອແຂນສັ້ນ	short-sleeved shirt
gàa-la-wat	ກາລະວັດ	necktie
sǎai-ɛ̀ɛo	ສາຍແອວ	belt
kěm-mǔt	ເຂັມໝຸດ	pin, brooch
gɔ̀ɔp	ເກີບ	shoe
tǒng-dtìin	ຖົງຕີນ	sock
tǒng-mùu	ຖົງມື	glove
sòng-sɔ̀ɔn-kǎa-nyáao	ໂສ້ງຂ້ອນຂາຍາວ	panty hose
ga-bpoong	ກະໂປ່ງ	skirt
sòng	ໂສ້ງ	trousers
dtûm-hǔu	ຕຸ້ມຫູ	earring
wɛ̌ɛn	ແຫວນ	ring
gông-kɛ̌ɛn/sǎai-kɛ̌ɛn	ກ້ອງແຂນ/ສາຍແຂນ	bracelet
sɔ̀i-kɔ̌ɔ/sǎai-kɔ̌ɔ	ສາຍສ້ອຍ/ສາຍຄໍ	necklace
bòo	ໂບ	ribbon
kɔ̌ɔng/kừang	ຂອງ/ເຄື່ອງ	thing
dtɛ̀ɛ-la/dtɔɔ	ແຕ່ລະ/ຕໍ່	per
kâap/kâng	ຄາບ/ຄັ້ງ	time
bpèn-nyǎng	ເປັນຫຍັງ?	"What's the matter?"
kóng/kóng-jǎ/kừu-sì	ຄົງ/ຄົງຈະ/ຄືຊິ	may, maybe

Conversation

Ron: ma-nîi sà-baai-dii bɔɔ.

ຣອນ: ມະນີ,   ສະບາຍດີ   ບໍ່?

Manee, how are you doing?

Manee: kɔ̀i bɔɔ kɔi sa-bàai bpàan-dǎi.*

ມະນີ:   ຂ້ອຍ ບໍ່ ຄ່ອຍ ສະບາຍ ປານໃດ.

I'm not so well. (*Not so much.)

Ron: bpèn-nyǎng.

ຣອນ: ເປັນຫຍັງ.

What's the matter?

Manee: mûu-nîi kɔ̀i jěp hǔa lǎai. kit waa kʉ́ʉ si bpèn wǎt.

ມະນີ:   ມື້ນີ້   ຂ້ອຍ ເຈັບ ຫົວ ຫລາຍ. ຄິດ ວ່າ   ຄື ຊິ ເປັນ ຫວັດ.

Today I have a bad headache. I think I may have a cold.

Ron: jâo bpài hóong-mɔ̌ɔ lɛ̂ɛo bɔɔ.

ຣອນ: ເຈົ້າ ໄປ   ໂຮງໝໍ   ແລ້ວ ບໍ່.

Have you gone to see a doctor (to the hospital)?

Manee: nyáng-tʉa. kit-waa mûu-ʉ̀ʉn jʉng** ja bpài.

ມະນີ:   ຍັງເທື່ອ.   ຄິດວ່າ ມື້ອື່ນ   ຈຶ່ງ   ຈະ ໄປ.

Not yet. I will go tomorrow.

(** jʉng is used for emphasis.)

táan lɔ́ɔn sa-bàai dìi bɔɔ.

ທ່ານ ຣອນ   ສະບາຍ ດີ ບໍ່?

How are you doing, Ron?

Ron: sa-bàai dìi. dtɛɛ-waa àa-tit lɛ̂ɛo jěp kɛ̀o nɔ̀i-nʉng.

ຣອນ: ສະບາຍ ດີ.   ແຕ່ວ່າ   ອາທິດ ແລ້ວ ເຈັບ ແຂ້ວ ໜ້ອຍໜຶ່ງ.

I'm fine. But last week I had a little bit of a toothache.

Manee: mûu-nîi jâo ja het nyǎng.

ມະນີ:   ມື້ນີ້   ເຈົ້າ ຈະ ເຮັດ ຫຍັງ?

What will you do today?

Ron: kɔ̀i ja bpài sûu-kʉang yuu ta-làat sâo.***

ຣອນ: ຂ້ອຍ ຈະ   ໄປ   ຊື້ເຄື່ອງ   ຢູ່   ຕະຫລາດເຊົ້າ.

I will go shopping at Morning Market .

(*** Main shopping area of Vientiene.)

Manee: jâo ja sûu nyǎng.

ມະນີ:   ເຈົ້າ ຈະ   ຊື້   ຫຍັງ.

What will you buy?

Ron: kɔ̀i yàak sûu sʉa gǎp gɔ̀əp.

ຣອນ: ຂ້ອຍ ຢາກ   ຊື້   ເສື້ອ ກັບ   ເກີບ.

I want to buy shirts and shoes.

bpà-nyòok   ປະໂຫຍກ   Sentences

1. A: pûak-háo gamlang nung sùa yuu.

     ພວກ ເຮົາ   ກຳລັງ   ນຸ່ງ   ເສື້ອ ຍູ່.

     We are wearing (putting on) our shirts.

    B: láao nung sùa-nyai sǐi fâa-gɛɛ lɛ mat-gàa-la-wat sǐi dɛ̀ɛng.

     ລາວ ນຸ່ງ   ເສື້ອໃຫຍ່   ສີ   ຟ້າແກ່ ແລະ ມັກກາລະວັດ   ສີ ແດງ.

     He is wearing a blue business jacket and a red necktie.

2. A: láao nung sùa sǐi nyǎng.

     ລາວ ນຸ່ງ   ເສື້ອ ສີ   ຫຍັງ?

     What color shirt is he wearing?

    B: láao nung sùa sǐi kǎao.

     ລາວ ນຸ່ງ   ເສື້ອ ສີ ຂາວ.

     He is wearing a white shirt.

3.   mûu-ùun kɔ̀i ja bpài dtǎt pǒm.

     ມື້ອື່ນ   ຂ້ອຍ ຈະ ໄປ   ຕັດ ຜົມ.

     Tomorrow I will go get a haircut.

4.   kɔ̀i tɛ̌ɛ nùat tuk sâo.

     ຂ້ອຍ ແຖ ໜວດ ທຸກ ເຊົ້າ.

     I shave my mustache every morning.

5.   kón láao mak àap-nâm.

     ຄົນ ລາວ ມັກ   ອາບນ້ຳ.

     Lao people like to take baths.

6. A: jâo gìn kào mûu la jǎk kâap.

     ເຈົ້າ ກິນ ເຂົ້າ   ມື້ ລະ ຈັກ ຄາບ?

     How many times a day do you eat a meal?

    B: kɔ̀i gìn kào mûu la sǎam kâap.

     ຂ້ອຍ ກິນ ເຂົ້າ   ມື້ ລະ ສາມ ຄາບ.

     I eat three times a day.

7. A: jâo sak-kʉang-nung àa-tit la jǎk tʉa.

    ເຈົ້າ ຊັກເຄື່ອງນຸ່ງ   ອາທິດ ລະ ຈັກ ເທື່ອ?

    How many times a week do you do the laundry?

  B: kɔ̀i sak-kʉang-nung àa-tit la sɔ̌ɔng tʉa.

    ຂ້ອຍ   ຊັກເຄື່ອງນຸ່ງ   ອາທິດ ລະ ສອງ ເທື່ອ.

    I do the laundry twice a week.

8.   mʉ̂ʉ-nîi kɔ̀i jěp kὲo lǎai tὲε-tὲε.

    ມື້ນີ້ ຂ້ອຍ ເຈັບ ແຂ້ວ ຫລາຍ ແທ້ໆ.

    Today I really have a bad toothache.

9.   kɔ̀i ja bpài lâang mʉ́ʉ yuu hɔ̀ng-nâm.

    ຂ້ອຍ ຈະ ໄປ   ລ້າງ   ມື ຢູ່   ຫ້ອງນ້ຳ.

    I will go wash my hands in the bathroom.

10.   kɔ̀i yàak mîi nùat.

    ຂ້ອຍ ຢາກ ມີ ໜວດ.

    I want to have a mustache.

11.   jěp hǔa-kao.

    ເຈັບ ຫົວເຂົ່າ.

    My knees hurt.

12.   pûak-háo mîi nîu-mʉ́ʉ hàa nîu.

    ພວກເຮົາ ມີ   ນິ້ວມື   ຫ້າ ນິ້ວ.

    We have five fingers.

13.   kɔ̀i ja bpài sʉ̀ʉ sa-bùu gǎp yàa-sǐi-kὲo.

    ຂ້ອຍ ຈະ ໄປ   ຊື້   ສະບູ   ກັບ ຢາສີແຂ້ວ.

    I will go to buy soap and toothpaste.

14.   láao mak nung sʉ̀a-kὲεn-nyáao.

    ລາວ ມັກ   ນຸ່ງ   ເສື້ອແຂນຍາວ.

    He likes to wear long sleeved shirts.

15.   tɔ́ɔng láao nyai nɔ̀i-nʉng.

    ທ້ອງ ລາວ ໃຫຍ່ ໜ້ອຍໜຶ່ງ.

    He has a little paunch.

Test 8

Match the English words with the Lao words.

_____ 1. hand   a. gə̀əp   ກີບ

_____ 2. to wash   b. hǔu   ຫູ

_____ 3. face   c. kǎa   ຂາ

_____ 4. to take a bath   d. múu   ມື

_____ 5. head   e. hǔa   ຫົວ

_____ 6. to cut   f. jěp   ເຈັບ

_____ 7. leg   g. ga-bpoong   ກະໂປ່ງ

_____ 8. shoe   h. àap-nâam   ອາບນ້ຳ

_____ 9. skirt   i. nàa   ໜ້າ

_____ 10. hair   j. sak-kʉang-nung   ຊັກເຄື່ອງນຸ່ງ

_____ 11. hat   k. mùak   ໝວກ

_____ 12. ear   l. sa-bùu   ສະບູ

_____ 13. soap   m. lâang   ລ້າງ

_____ 14. to do the laundry   n. pǒm   ຜົມ

_____ 15. to have pain   o. tǒng-dtìin   ຖົງຕີນ

                                   p. dtǎt   ຕັດ

                                   q. sòng   ໂສ້ງ

Translate the following into English.

1. A: jâo tǔu kὲo wán la jǎk tɯa.

    ເຈົ້າ ຖຸ ແຂ້ວ ວັນ ລະ ຈັກ ເທື່ອ.

    B: wán la sɔ̌ɔng tɯa.

    ວັນ ລະ ສອງ ເທື່ອ.

2. láao jĕp hǔa lǎai. láao máa het wîak bɔɔ dâi.

    ລາວ ເຈັບ ຫົວ ຫລາຍ. ລາວ ມາ ເຮັດ ວຽກ ບໍ່ ໄດ້.

3. kɔ̀i sǎ-pǒm tuk mɯ̂ɯ.

    ຂ້ອຍ ສະຜົມ ທຸກ ມື້.

4. sǒm-sǔk mɨ́i gȇεm-bɔng.

    ສົມສຸກ ມີ ແກ້ມບ່ອງ.

5. jâo bɔɔ mɨ́i sa-mɔ̌ɔng.

    ເຈົ້າ ບໍ່ ມີ ສະໝອງ.

Silent ຫ

A silent ຫ is called "hɔ̌ɔ-nám". It may appear before the following six low consonants. In this case, the low consonant takes on all the tone characteristics of the high consonant ຫ. When a tone mark appears, it is placed over the low consonant, not over the silent ຫ.

1. ງ (ຫງ)

2. ຍ (ຫຍ)

3. ນ (ໜ or ຫນ)

4. ມ (ໝ or ຫມ)

5. ລ (ຫຼ or ຫລ)

6. ວ (ຫວ)

		Sound Produced		Meaning
ຫ	+ ງອກ	= ຫງອກ (ngɔ̀ɔk)		gray hair
ຫ	+ ຍ້າ	= ຫຍ້າ (yàa)		grass
ຫ	+ ນີ້	= ໜີ້ (nìi)		debt
ຫ	+ ມາ	= ໝາ (mǎa)		dog
ຫ	+ ລາຍ	= ຫຼາຍ, ຫລາຍ (lǎai)		many
ຫ	+ ວ່ານ	= ຫວ່ານ (waan)		to sow

In syllables with the silent high consonant ຫ, all high consonant tone rules apply. (See pages 102 and 121.)

Tone Mark	Tone Name	Tone	Examples
None	sĭang jàt-dtà-waa	rising	ຫມາ (mǎa)
◌̀	sĭang sǎa-mán	mid	ຫມ່າ (maa)
◌̌	sĭang èek	low	ຫມ້າ (màa)

Exercise: Read the Following Words and Practice Writing Them in Lao. Also Identify the Tones.

1. ຫູ້ or

2. ໂຫລ dozen

3. ຫມູ rat

4. ຫມູ pig

5. ຫມ້າ face

6. ຫວານ sweet

7. ຫມອນ pillow

8. ຫລັບ asleep

9. ຫຍັງ what

10. ຫງາຍ face up

Read The Following Aloud

1. ໝ່າ   ໝ້າ   ໝາ

2. ໝິ່   ໝິ້   ໝິ

3. ແໝ່ງ   ແໝ້ງ   ແໝງ

4. ໄໝ່ລ   ໄໝ້ລ   ໄໝລ

5. ແໝ່ວາ   ແໝ້ວາ   ແໝວາ

6. ທຍ່າ   ທຍ້າ   ທຍາ

Writing Exercise 8

Transcribe the following into Lao script using ທ ນໍາ /hɔ̌ɔ-nám/.

1. mii _____   6. lǎa _____

2. nǎi _____   7. wuu _____

3. yai _____   8. long _____

4. ǹii _____   9. wan _____

5. man _____   10. wǎa _____

Lesson 9

family and kinship terms; occupations; animals;
punctuation marks; practice reading short sentences

bŏt-tii gâo   ບົດທີ ເກົ້າ   Lesson 9
kám-săp   ຄຳສັບ   Vocabulary

sŭan ສວນ	garden
sŭan-săt ສວນສັດ	zoo
àa-nyu ອາຍຸ	age
bɔɔ-li-săt ບໍລິສັດ	company
bpèn nyăng ເປັນຫຍັງ	why
pɔ-waa/nyɔ̂ɔn-wâa ເພາະວ່າ/ຍ້ອນວ່າ	because
tàa/tàa-hàak ຖ້າ/ຖ້າຫາກ	if
dtɛng-ngáan/dtɛng-dɔ̀ɔng	to get married, to marry
ແຕ່ງງານ/ແຕ່ງດອງ	
sòot ໂສດ	single
hak ຮັກ	to love
táng-sɔ̌ɔng ທັງສອງ	both

kɔ̂p-kúa   ຄອບຄົວ   Family

puu-sáai ຜູ້ຊາຍ	man, male
puu-nyíng ຜູ້ຍິງ	woman, female
puu-nyai ຜູ້ໃຫຍ່	adult
dĕk-nɔ̂ɔi/lûuk ເດັກນ້ອຍ/ລູກ	child
lûuk-sáai ລູກຊາຍ	son
lûuk-săao ລູກສາວ	daughter
săa-míi ສາມິ	husband
pán-la-nyáa ພັນລະຍາ	wife
pŭa ຜົວ	husband
mía ເມຍ/ເມັຽ	wife

pɔɔ	ພໍ່	father
mɛɛ	ແມ່	mother
âai-ûai	ອ້າຍເອື້ອຍ	older sibling
nɔ̂ɔng	ນ້ອງ	younger sibling
âai	ອ້າຍ	older brother
ûai	ເອື້ອຍ	older sister
nɔ̂ɔng-sáai	ນ້ອງຊາຍ	younger brother
nɔ̂ɔng-săao	ນ້ອງສາວ	younger sister
bpuu	ປູ່	father's father
nyaa	ຍ່າ	father's mother
pɔɔ-tào	ພໍ່ເຖົ້າ	mother's father
mɛɛ-tào	ແມ່ເຖົ້າ	mother's mother
lúng	ລຸງ	father or mother's older brother
bpâa	ປ້າ	father or mother's older sister
nâa-baao/nâa-săao	ນ້າບ່າວ/ນ້າສາວ	mother's younger brother or sister
àao	ອາວ	father's younger brother
àa	ອາ	father's younger sister

àa-sîip ອາຊີບ Occupations

kuu/àa-jàan	ຄູ/ອາຈານ	teacher, professor
taan-mɔ̌ɔ	ທ່ານໝໍ	doctor
(taan)-mɔ̌ɔ-bpùa-kɛo	(ທ່ານ)ໝໍປົວແຂ້ວ	dentist
nak-tu-la-gǐt	ນັກທຸລະກິດ	businessman
nak-sǔk-săa	ນັກສຶກສາ	college student

nak-hían ນັກຮຽນ   student
nak-kían ນັກຂຽນ   writer
nak-bìn ນັກບິນ   pilot
nak-hɔ̂ɔng ນັກຮ້ອງ   singer
nak-sùup ນັກສືບ   spy
nak-ɔ̀ɔk-bὲɛp ນັກອອກແບບ   designer
pa-nak-ngáan-lat ພະນັກງານລັດ   government official
wit-sa-wa-gɔ̀ɔn ວິສະວະກອນ   engineer
dtàm-lùat ຕຳຫລວດ   policeman
ta-hǎan ທະຫານ   soldier
pa-nyàa-bàan ພະຍາບານ   nurse
kón-kǎp-lot ຄົນຂັບລົດ   driver
saang-(jǎk) ຊ່າງ (ຈັກ)   mechanic
saang-dtǎt-pǒm ຊ່າງຕັດຜົມ   barber
sáao-náa ຊາວນາ   farmer
pa/kúu-bàa ພະ/ຄຸບາ   monk
lée-kǎa ເລຂາ   secretary
mɛɛ-bâan/mɛɛ-hǔan   housewife
ແມ່ບ້ານ/ ແມ່ເຮືອນ
pɔɔ-kâa/mɛɛ-kâa ພໍຄ້າ/ ແມ່ຄ້າ   merchant
dàa-láa ດາລາ   movie star
jâo-kɔ̌ɔng ເຈົ້າຂອງ   owner
jâo-kɔ̌ɔng-hâan ເຈົ້າຂອງຮ້ານ   shop owner
jâo-kɔ̌ɔng tu-la-gìt ເຈົ້າຂອງທຸລະກິດ   business owner
het-wîak kɔ̌ɔng dtòn-èeng   self-employed
ເຮັດວຽກຂອງຕົນເອງ
het-wîak bɔ̀ɔ-li-sǎt ເຮັດວຽກບໍລິສັດ   company employee
nak-bpûn/jòon-bpûn ນັກປຸ້ນ/ໂຈນປຸ້ນ   robber
ka-móoi/jòon/kón-kìi-lak   thief
ຂະໂມຍ/ໂຈນ/ຄົນຂີ້ລັກ

săt ສັດ **Animals**

săt-ĺiang	ສັດລ້ຽງ	pet
dtòo-pùu/dtòo-tɔ̀ək	ໂຕຜູ້/ໂຕເຖິກ	male (animal)
dtòo-mɛɛ	ໂຕແມ່	female (animal)
mǎa	ໝາ	dog
mɛ́ɛo	ແມວ	cat
mǔu	ໝູ	pig
bpět	ເປັດ	duck
gai/gai-mɛɛ	ໄກ່/ໄກ່ແມ່	chicken, hen
sâang	ຊ້າງ	elephant
mâa	ມ້າ	horse
ngúa	ງົວ	cow, ox
kwáai	ຄວາຍ	buffalo
bpùu	ປູ	crab
bpàa	ປາ	fish
hɔ̌i	ຫອຍ	shell, oyster, etc.
gûng	ກຸ້ງ	shrimp
nok	ນົກ	bird
ĺing	ລີງ	monkey
nǔu	ໜູ	rat, mouse
ngúu	ງູ	snake
sǔa	ເສືອ	tiger
sǐng-dtòo	ສິງໂຕ	lion
kɛ̀ɛ	ແຂ້	crocodile
dtao	ເຕົ່າ	turtle
dtoo-jing-jôo	ໂຕຈິງໂຈ້	kangaroo
bɛ̂ɛ	ແບ້	goat
gɛ̌	ແກະ	sheep
mǐi	ໝີ	bear
ùut	ອູດ	camel

jia	ຈັຽ	bat
mâa-láai	ມ້າລາຍ	zebra
mǎa-bpaa/mǎa-nái	ໝາປ່າ/ໝາໄມ	wolf
mǎa-jɔ̀ɔk	ໝາຈອກ	fox
mɛ́ɛng-ga-bûa	ແມງກະເບື້ອ	butterfly
mot	ມົດ	ant
nyúng	ຍຸງ	mosquito
mɛ́ɛng-wán	ແມງວັນ	fly

Conversation

Ann: kúun, jâo dtɛng-ngáan lɛ́ɛo bɔɔ.

ແອນ: ຄູນ, ເຈົ້າ ແຕ່ງງານ ແລ້ວ ບໍ?

Kuun, are you married?

Kuun: dtɛng lɛ̂ɛo. mía kɔ̀i sɯɯ wî-lái.

ຄູນ: ແຕ່ງ ແລ້ວ. ເມຍ ຂ້ອຍ ຊື່ ວິໄລ.

Yes. My wife's name is Wilai.

Ann: jâo míi lûuk lɛ̂ɛo bɔɔ.

ແອນ: ເຈົ້າ ມີ ລູກ ແລ້ວ ບໍ?

Do you have children?

Kuun: míi lɛ́ɛo, sɔ̌ɔng kón. nyíng nɯng, sáai nɯng.

ຄູນ: ມີ ແລ້ວ. ສອງ ຄົນ, ຍິງ ໜຶ່ງ, ຊາຍ ໜຶ່ງ.

I have two, one girl and one boy.

Ann: jâo het wîak nyǎng.

ແອນ: ເຈົ້າ ເຮັດ ວຽກ ຫຍັງ?

What kind of work do you do?

Kuun: kɔ̀i het wîak yuu ta-náa-káan.

ຄູນ: ຂ້ອຍ ເຮັດ ວຽກ ຢູ່ ທະນາຄານ.

I work at a bank.

Ann: ta-náa-káan dǎi.

ແອນ: ທະນາຄານ ໃດ?

What bank?

Kuun: ta-náa-káan láao-mai.

ຄູນ: ທະນາຄານ   ລາວໃໝ່.

New Laos Bank.

ɛ̀ɛn, jâo het wîak nyǎng.

ແອນ, ເຈົ້າ ເຮັດ ວຽກ ຫຍັງ?

What kind of work do you do, Ann?

Ann: kɔ̀i het tu-la-gǐt kɔ̌ɔng kɔ̀i eeng yuu àa-mée-li-gàa.

ແອນ: ຂ້ອຍ ເຮັດ ຫຸລະກິດ ຂອງ ຂ້ອຍ ເອງ ຢູ່ ອາເມລິກາ.

I work for myself in America.

Kuun: jâo dtɛng-ngáan lɛ̂ɛo bɔɔ.

ຄູນ: ເຈົ້າ ແຕ່ງງານ ແລ້ວ ບໍ່?

Are you married?

Ann: nyáng. kɔ̀i nyáng bɔɔ tán mǐi fɛ́ɛn tʉa.

ແອນ: ຍັງ.   ຂ້ອຍ ຍັງ ບໍ່ ທັນ ມີ ແຟນ ເທື່ອ.

Not yet. I don't have a boyfriend yet.

bpà-nyòok ປະໂຫຍກ **Sentences**

1. A: kɔ̀ɔp-kúa jâo míi jăk kón.

   ຄອບ ຄົວ ເຈົ້າ ມີ ຈັກ ຄົນ?

   How many people are there in your family?

   B: míi jĕt kón. míi pɔɔ, mɛɛ, âai, ûai,

   ມີ ເຈັດ ຄົນ. ມີ ພໍ່, ແມ່, ອ້າຍ, ເອື້ອຍ.

   nɔ̀ɔng-sáai sɔ̌ɔng kón gǎp kɔ̀i.

   ນ້ອງຊາຍ ສອງ ຄົນ ກັບ ຂ້ອຍ.

   There are seven — my father, mother, older brother,
   older sister, two younger brothers and me.

2. A: puu-nân mɛɛn pǎi.

   ຜູ້ນັ້ນ ແມ່ນ ໃຜ?

   Who is that?

   B: puu-nân mɛɛn nɔ̀ɔng-sǎao kɔ̀i.

   ຜູ້ນັ້ນ ແມ່ນ ນ້ອງສາວ ຂ້ອຍ.

   That is my younger sister.

3. A: âai jâo het wîak nyǎng.

   ອ້າຍ ເຈົ້າ ເຮັດ ວຽກ ຫຍັງ?

   What kind of work does your older brother do?

   B: láao bpèn witsa-wa-gɔ̀ɔn.

   ລາວ ເປັນ ວິສະວະກອນ.

   He is an engineer.

   A: jâo het wîak nyǎng.

   ເຈົ້າ ເຮັດ ວຽກ ຫຍັງ?

   What kind of work do you do?

B: kɔ̀i het wîak yuu bɔ̀ɔ-li-sǎt.

ຂ້ອຍ ເຮັດ ວຽກ ຢູ່ ບໍລິສັດ.

I work for a company.

4. A: láao het wîak nyǎng.

ລາວ ເຮັດ ວຽກ ຫຍັງ?

What is his occupation?

B: láao bpèn kúu sɔ̌ɔn páa-sǎa láao.

ລາວ ເປັນ ຄູ ສອນ ພາສາ ລາວ.

He is a Lao teacher.

5. A: jâo dtɛng-ngáan lɛ̂ɛo bɔɔ.

ເຈົ້າ ແຕ່ງງານ ແລ້ວ ບໍ?

Are you married yet?

B: dtɛ̀ng lɛ̂ɛo.

ແຕ່ງ ແລ້ວ.

Yes, I am.

C: nyáng, nýang bɔɔ tán dtɛng. kɔ̀i nyáng bpen sòot yuu.

ຍັງ, ຍັງ ບໍ່ ທັນ ແຕ່ງ. ຂ້ອຍ ຍັງ ເປັນ ໂສດ ຢູ່.

No, I'm not. I'm still single.

6. A: jâo míi lûuk jǎk kón.

ເຈົ້າ ມີ ລູກ ຈັກ ຄົນ?

How many children do you have?

B: sɔ̌ɔng kón.   bpèn puu-sáai táng sɔ̌ɔng kón.

ສອງ ຄົນ. ເປັນ ຜູ້ຊາຍ ທັງ ສອງ ຄົນ.

Two. Both of them are boys.

7. A: jâo àa-nyu tao-dǎi. / jâo àa-nyu jǎk bpìi.

ເຈົ້າ ອາຍ ເທົ່າໃດ?/ ເຈົ້າ ອາຍຸ ຈັກ ປີ?

How old are you?

B: sǎam-sǐp bpìi.

ສາມສິບ   ປີ.

Thirty years old.

A: ûai jâo àa-nyu tao-dǎi.

ເອື້ອຍ ເຈົ້າ ອາຍຸ ເທົ່າໃດ?

How old is your older sister?

B: sǎam-sǐp-sii.

ສາມສິບສີ່.

Thirty-four.

8. A: hûan jâo míi sǎt-lîing bɔɔ.

ເຮືອນ ເຈົ້າ ມີ   ສັດລ້ຽງ ບໍ?

Do you have pets at home?

B: míi.   míi mǎa gǎp mɛ́ɛo.

ມີ.   ມີ   ໝາ ກັບ ແມວ.

Yes, I have a dog and a cat.

9. A: pǎi bpèn kúu sɔ̌ɔn páa-sǎa láao.

ໃຜ ເປັນ ຄູ ສອນ   ພາສາ   ລາວ?

Who is the Lao teacher?

B: taan sɔ̌ɔn bpèn kúu sɔ̌ɔn páa-sǎa láao.

ທ່ານ ສອນ ເປັນ ຄູ   ສອນ   ພາສາ ລາວ.

Mr. Sorn is the Lao teacher.

10. A: jâo het wîak gǎp bɔɔ-li-sǎt nyǎng.

ເຈົ້າ ເຮັດ ວຽກ ກັບ   ບໍລິສັກ   ຫຍັງ?

What company do you work with?

B: het gǎp bɔɔ-li-sǎt nyii-bpun.

ເຮັດ ກັບ ບໍລິສັກ   ຍີ່ປຸ່ນ.

With a Japanese company.

11. A: bpèn nyăng jâo jɨng hían páa-săa láao.

ເປັນ ຫຍັງ ເຈົ້າ ຈຶ່ງ ຮຽນ ພາສາ ລາວ?

Why do you study Lao?

B: pɔ-waa kɔ̀i mak kón láao lăai.

ເພາະວ່າ ຂ້ອຍ ມັກ ຄົນ ລາວ ຫລາຍ.

Because I like Lao people very much.

12. A: àa-tit lɛ̂ɛo bpèn nyăng jâo jɨng bɔɔ máa wat.

ອາທິດ ແລ້ວ ເປັນ ຫຍັງ ເຈົ້າ ຈຶ່ງ ບໍ່ ມາ ວັດ?

Why didn't you come to the temple last week?

B: prɔ-waa kɔ̀i bɔɔ kɔi sa-bàai.

ເພາະວ່າ ຂ້ອຍ ບໍ່ ຄ່ອຍ ສະບາຍ.

Because I wasn't feeling well.

13. A: tàa jâo míi ngán lăai lăai, jâo yàak ja het nyăng.

ຖ້າ ເຈົ້າ ມີ ເງິນ ຫລາຍໆ, ເຈົ້າ ຍາກ ຈະ ເຮັດ ຫຍັງ?

If you had a lot of money, what would you do?

B: kɔ̀i ja sɨ̂ɨ húan yuu mɨ́ang láao.

ຂ້ອຍ ຈະ ຊື້ ເຮືອນ ຢູ່ ເມືອງ ລາວ.

I would buy a house in Laos.

14. A: tàa fŏn dtŏk, jâo ja het jang dǎi.

ຖ້າ ຝົນ ຕົກ ເຈົ້າ ຈະ ເຮັດ ຈັ່ງ ໃດ?

If it rains, what (how) will you do?

B: kɔ̀i gɔɔ ja bɔɔ bpài het wîak.

ຂ້ອຍ ກໍ່ ຈະ ບໍ່ ໄປ ເຮັດ ວຽກ.

I won't go to work.

15.   mɨ̀ɨ-nîi kɔ̀i jĕp kɛ̀o lăai. kɔ̀i yàak bpài-hăa mɔ̌ɔ-bpua-kɛ̀o.

ມື້ນີ້ ຂ້ອຍ ເຈັບ ແຂ້ວ ຫລາຍ. ຂ້ອຍ ຍາກ ໄປຫາ ໝໍປົວແຂ້ວ.

Today I have a bad toothache. I want to. see a dentist.

16.   kɔ̌i kit waa láao bpèn nak tu-la-gǐt jàak nyii-bpun.

ຂ້ອຍ ຄິດ ວ່າ ລາວ ເປັນ ນັກ ທຸລະກິດ ຈາກ ຍີ່ປຸ່ນ.

I think he is a businessman from Japan.

17.   yuu nìi míi jòon lǎai têɛ-têɛ.

ຢູ່ ນີ້ ມີ ໂຈນ ຫລາຍ ແທ້ໆ.

This place really has a lot of thieves.

18. A: kɔ̌i míi lúng yuu tii àng-gǐt.

ຂ້ອຍ ມີ ລຸງ ຢູ່ ທີ່ ອັງກິດ.

I have an uncle in England.

   B: láao míi kɔ̌ɔp-kúa yuu tii múang-láao.

ລາວ ມີ ຄອບຄົວ ຢູ່ ທີ່ ເມືອງລາວ.

He has a family in Laos.

19. A: kɔ̌i yàak dtɛng-ngáan gǎp jâo.

ຂ້ອຍ ຢາກ ແຕ່ງງານ ກັບ ເຈົ້າ.

I want to marry you.

   B: láao yàak dtɛng-ngáan gǎp kón láao.

ລາວ ຢາກ ແຕ່ງງານ ກັບ ຄົນ ລາວ.

He wants to marry a Laotian.

20. A: kɔ̌i hak jâo lǎai.

ຂ້ອຍ ຮັກ ເຈົ້າ ຫລາຍ.

I love you very much.

   B: láao hak kɔ̌ɔp-kúa lǎai.

ລາວ ຮັກ ຄອບຄົວ ຫລາຍ.

He loves his family very much.

   C: kɔ̌i hak múang-láao.

ຂ້ອຍ ຮັກ ເມືອງລາວ.

I love Laos.

Test 9

Match the English words with the Lao words.

A   Family

_____ 1. uncle   a. nɔ̂ɔng-sǎao   ນ້ອງສາວ

_____ 2. grandfather   b. mia   ເມຍ

_____ 3. daughter   c. lung   ລຸງ

_____ 4. younger brother   d. lûuk-sǎao   ລູກສາວ

_____ 5. grandmother   e. bpuu   ປູ່

_____ 6. aunt   f. pǔa   ຜົວ

_____ 7. son   g. âai   ອ້າຍ

_____ 8. husband   h. lûuk-sáai   ລູກຊາຍ

_____ 9. wife   i. mɛɛ   ແມ່

_____ 10. older sister   j. n̂ai   ເອື້ອຍ

                               k. nɔ̂ɔng-sáai   ນ້ອງຊາຍ

                               l. bpâa   ປ້າ

                               m. nyaa   ຍ່າ

B   Occupations

_____ 1. dentist   a. nak-bìn   ນັກບິນ

_____ 2. soldier   b. wit-sa-wa-gɔɔn   ວິສະວະກອນ

_____ 3. nurse   c. pa-nyáa-bàan/náai-mɔ̌ɔ

                                 ພະຍາບານ/ນາຍໝໍ

_____ 4. farmer   d. nak-hían   ນັກຮຽນ

_____ 5. movie star   e. dtàm-lùat   ຕຳຫລວດ

_____ 6. police   f. nak-hɔ̂ɔng   ນັກຮ້ອງ

_____ 7. student   g. dàa-láa   ດາລາ

_____ 8. singer   h. mɔ̌ɔ-bpùa-kɛ̀o   ໝໍປົວແຂ້ວ

_____ 9. engineer   i. àa-jàan   ອາຈານ

_____ 10. pilot   j. ta-hǎan   ທະຫານ

                               k. nak-kǐan   ນັກຂຽນ

                               l. sáao-náa   ຊາວນາ

                               m. nak-tu-ra-gǐt   ນັກທຸລະກິດ

C   Animals

_____ 1. pig		a. nǔu	ໝູ
_____ 2. fish		b. mâa	ມ້າ
_____ 3. bird		c. kǎa	ຂາ
_____ 4. horse		d. gai	ໄກ່
_____ 5. monkey		e. sǔa	ເສືອ
_____ 6. tiger		f. bpàa	ປາ
_____ 7. dog		g. kwáai	ຄວາຍ
_____ 8. shrimp		h. gûng	ກຸ້ງ
_____ 9. elephant		i. mǎa	ໝາ
_____ 10. buffalo		j. líng	ລິງ
		k. mǔu	ໝູ
		l. nok	ນົກ
		m. sâang	ຊ້າງ

Translate the following into English.

1. _A:_ nɔ̂ɔng sáai jâo het wîak nyǎng.
   ນ້ອງ ຊາຍ ເຈົ້າ ເຮັດ ວຽກ ຫຍັງ?

_____

2. láao dtɛng-ngáan gǎp kón nyii-bpun.
   ລາວ   ແຕ່ງງານ   ກັບ ຄົນ ຍີ່ປຸ່ນ.

_____

3. _A:_ bpèn nyǎng jâo jɨng bɔɔ mak àa-hǎan láao.
   ເປັນ   ຫຍັງ ເຈົ້າ ຈຶ່ງ ບໍ່ ມັກ ອາຫານ ລາວ?

   _B:_ prɔ-waa mán pět lǎai.
   ເພາະ ວ່າ ມັນ ເຜັດ ຫລາຍ.

_____

4. tàa bɔɔ míi ngớn gɔɔ ja gǎp mɨang-láao bɔɔ dâi.
   ຖ້າ ບໍ່ ມີ ເງິນ ກໍ່ ຈະ ກັບ   ເມືອງລາວ ບໍ່ ໄດ້.

_____

5. kɔ̀i kit waa láao míi kɔ̂ɔp-kúa lɛ̂ɛo.
   ຂ້ອຍ ຄຶດ ວ່າ ລາວ ມີ   ຄອບຄົວ   ແລ້ວ.

_____

Punctuation Marks

1. ເຄື່ອງໝາຍຈ້ຳ ⌊.⌋ /kɯang-mǎai-jâm/ is used at the end of a sentence or paragraph like the full stop or period in English.

2. ເຄື່ອງໝາຍຈຸດ ⌊,⌋ /kɯang-mǎai-jǔt/ is used like the comma in English.

3. ເຄື່ອງໝາຍຈ້ຳຈຸດ ⌊;⌋ /kɯang-mǎai-jâm-jǔt/ is used like the semi-colon in English.

4. ເຄື່ອງໝາຍສອງຈ້ຳ ⌊:⌋ /kɯang-mǎai-sɔ̌ɔng-jâm/ is used like the colon in English.

5. ເຄື່ອງໝາຍຂີດຕໍ່ ⌊-⌋ /kɯang-mǎai-kìit-dtɔɔ/ is used like the dash in English.

6. ເຄື່ອງໝາຍຂີດກ້ອງ ⌊＿＿＿⌋ /kɯang-mǎai-kìit-gɔ̂ng/ is used like the underline in English.

7. ເຄື່ອງໝາຍຈ້ຳໆ ⌊...⌋ /kɯang-mǎai-jâm-jâm/ is used to show that there are more items that are not mentioned.

8. ເຄື່ອງໝາຍຖາມ ⌊?⌋ /kɯang-mǎai-tǎam/ is used like the question mark in English.

9. ເຄື່ອງໝາຍທ້ວງ ⌊!⌋ /kɯang-mǎai-tûang/ is used like the exclamation mark in English.

10. ເຄື່ອງໝາຍວົງຢືມ ⌊" "⌋ /kɯang-mǎai-wóng-yɯɯm/ is used like the quotation mark in English.

11. ເຄື່ອງໝາຍວົງເລັບ ⌊( )⌋ /kɯang-mǎai-wóng-lep/ is used like the parentheses in English.

12. ເຄື່ອງໝາຍລ້ຳ ⌊„⌋ /kɯang-mǎai-lɯ̂m/ is used like the ditto mark in English.

13. ເຄື່ອງໝາຍ ແລະອື່ນໆ ⎡ງຯງ⎤ /kʉang-mǎai-le-ʉʉn-ʉʉn/ is used like the "etc.," in English.

14. ເຄື່ອງໝາຍຊ້ຳ ⎡ງ ⎤ /kʉang-mǎai-sâm/ is used to indicate that the word or phrase is repeated for emphasis.

Other Symbols

ໄມ້ກັນ ⌣ /mâi-gàn/ is the short vowel −ະ /ǎ/. It is written in this form when the syllable has a final consonant.

For example:

ກະ gǎ   ກັນ gàn

It is also used to change the long vowels ເ- (èe) and ແ- (èɛ) into the short vowels ເ-ະ (ě) and ແ-ະ (ěɛ) when the syllable has a final consonant.

For example:

ເບນ bpèen   ເບັນ bpèn

ໄມ້ກົງ ⌢ /mâi-gòng/ goes between two characters to form a short /o/ sound.

For example:

ໂດນ kóon   ຄົນ kón

Reading Exercise

Read the following aloud and translate.

1. ເຈົ້າ ຢູ່ ໃສ?

2. ພາສາ ລາວ ບໍ່ ຍາກ.

3. ຂ້ອຍ ມັກ ສີຂາວ.

4. ລາວ ມີ ເຮືອນ ຫລັງ ງາມໆ.

5. ເຈົ້າ ສະບາຍ ດີບໍ່?

6. ຂ້ອຍ ເປັນ ຄົນລາວ.

7. ອັນນີ້ ລາຄາ ເທົ່າໃດ?

8. ທ່ານ ທານາກະ ເປັນ ຄົນຍີ່ປຸ່ນ.

9. ຫ້ອງນ້ຳ ຢູ່ໃສ?

10. ສໍ ຢູ່ ໃຕ້ ໂຕະ.

11. ໂຮງແຮມ ຢູ່ ທາງຂວາ.

12. ຄົນນັ້ນ ງາມ ອີ່ຫລີ.

13. ມື້ນີ້ ແມ່ນ ວັນຫຍັງ?

14. ມື້ນີ້ ແມ່ນ ວັນອາທິດ.

15. ລົດຍົນ ຂອງ ເຈົ້າ ສີຫຍັງ?

16. ຂ້ອຍ ໄປ ເຮັດວຽກ ຕອນເຊົ້າ.

17. ທ່ານ ສົມສຸກ ມັກ ເບິ່ງທີວີ/ໂທລະພາບ.

18. ພວກເຮົາ ຈະ ໄປ ກິນ ອາຫານລາວ.

19. ຄູວມີ ເວລາ ເທົ່າໃດ?

20. ຈະ ໄປ ຄິມ ເຮືອບິນ ຕອນ ສິບສອງໂມງ.

21. ເຈົ້າ ຈະ ໄປ ໃສ?

22. ຈະ ໄປ ຮຽນ ພາສາ ລາວ.

23. ຂ້ອຍ ບໍ່ ມັກ ອາຫານ ຈີນ.

24. ລາວ ມີ ໝາ ຢູ່ ເຮືອນ.

25. ຂ້ອຍ ຈະ ໄປ ເມືອງ ລາວ ເດືອນ ໜ້າ.

26. ວັນຈັນ ໜ້າ ຂ້ອຍ ຈະ ບໍ່ ຢູ່.

27. ພວກເຮົາ ຈະ ໄປ ຮຽນ ພາສາ ອັງກິດ ຢູ່ ທີ່
    ອາເມລິກາ.

28. ຄົນ ຍີ່ປຸ່ນ ມັກ ເຮັດ ວຽກ.

29. ຂ້ອຍ ປາກ ເວົ້າ ທ້ອງນ້ຳ.

30. ເຈົ້າ ກຳລັງ ເຮັດ ຫຍັງ?

31. ທ່ານ ຈອນ ປາກ ພາສາ ຈີນ ໄດ້.

32. ມີມີ ເມື່ອຍ ອິຫລີ.

33. ອັນນີ້ ແມ່ນ ໜັງສື ຂອງ ໃຜ?

34. ມີມີ ຮ້ອນ ຫລາຍ.

35. ຄົນຮັກ ເຈົ້າ ຊື່ ຫຍັງ?

36. ຂ້ອຍ ອາບນ້ຳ ທຸກວັນ.

37. ຂ້ອຍ ຊັກ ເຄື່ອງນຸ່ງ ທຸກ ວັນເສົາ.

38. ເຮົາ ບໍ່ ປາກ ຊື້ ເຄື່ອງ ແພງ.

39. ຄຣູນີ້ ເຈັບ ຫົວ ຫລາຍ.

40. ຂ້ອຍ ຖູ ແຂ້ວ ວັນ ລະ ສອງ ເທື່ອ.

Lesson 10

comparisons; adjectives; classifiers; practice reading
short sentences and paragraphs

bŏt-tíi sǐp   ບົດທີ ສິບ   Lesson 10

kám-sǎp   ຄຳສັບ   Vocabulary

gwaa/gua	ກວ່າ	than
tii-sǔt	ທີ່ສຸດ	most
dtɛɛ	ແຕ່	but
nyai	ໃຫຍ່	big
nɔ̂ɔi	ນ້ອຍ	small
dtûi	ຕຸ້ຍ	fat
jɔi	ຈ່ອຍ	thin
nǎa	ຫນາ	thick
bàang	ບາງ	thin
sǔung	ສູງ	tall, high (height)
dtîa/dtam	ເຕ້ຍ/ຕ່ຳ	short (height)
dtàm	ຕ່ຳ	low
nyáao	ຍາວ	long (measurement)
sàn	ສັ້ນ	short (measurement)
nǎk	ຫນັກ	heavy
bào	ເບົາ	light (weight)
gwâang	ກວ້າງ	wide
kɛ̂ɛp	ແຄບ	narrow
hɔ̂ɔn	ຮ້ອນ	hot
nǎao	ຫນາວ	cold (weather)
yen	ເຢັນ	cold, cool
lǎai	ຫລາຍ	much, many
nɔ̀i	ຫນ້ອຍ	little
gɛɛ/tào	ແກ່/ເຖົ້າ	old
num/ɔɔn	ຫນຸ່ມ/ອ່ອນ	young
mai	ໃຫມ່	new

gao	ເກົ່າ	old
kěng-héeng	ແຂງແຮງ	strong
ɔɔn-ὲɛ	ອ່ອນແອ	weak
sa-làat	ສະຫຼາດ	intelligent
ngoo	ໂງ່	stupid
jêɛng	ແຈ້ງ	bright, light
mûʉt	ມືດ	dark
gài	ໄກ	far
gâi	ໃກ້	near
àn-dta-láai	ອັນຕະລາຍ	dangerous
bpɔ̀ɔt-pái	ປອດໄພ	safe
bpèn-dtàa-yâan	ເປັນຕາຢ້ານ	awful, terrifying, scary
bpèn-dtàa-sǒn-jài	ເປັນຕາສົນໃຈ	interesting
bpèn-dtàa-bʉa	ເປັນຕາເບື່ອ	boring
sa-dùak	ສະດວກ	convenient
sa-bàai	ສະບາຍ	comfortable
sa-àat	ສະອາດ	clean
bpʉ̂an	ເປື້ອນ	dirty
nyùng	ຫຍຸ້ງ	busy
waang/bpao	ຫວ່າງ/ເປົ່າ	free, empty
ka-nyǎn	ຂະຫຍັນ	diligent
kîi-kâan	ຂີ້ຄ້ານ	lazy
hang-míi	ຣັ່ງມີ	rich
tuk/jòn	ທຸກ/ຈົນ	poor
ngáam	ງາມ	beautiful, pretty
bpèn-dtàa-hak	ເປັນຕາຮັກ	cute
jâo-sûu	ເຈົ້າຊູ້	handsome
míi-sʉʉ-sǐang	ມີຊື່ສຽງ	famous
sǎmkán	ສำຄັນ	important
pi-sèet	ພິເສດ	special

kìi-tii ຂີ້ຖີ່   thrifty, cheap

dìi-jài ດີໃຈ   glad

jài-dìi ໃຈດີ   kind

jài-gwâang ໃຈກວ້າງ   generous

jài-yèn ໃຈເຢັນ   calm

jài-hɔ̂ɔn ໃຈຮ້ອນ   impatient

sua ຊົ່ວ   bad

ngîap/mit ງຽບ/ມິດ   quiet

kɔ̆ɔ ຂໍ   to ask for something

sùup ສູບ   to smoke

gìat-sáng/sáng ກຽດຊັງ/ຊັງ   to hate

kìi-dtŭa ຂີ້ຕົວະ   to lie

lôok ໂລກ   earth, world

láa-káa ລາຄາ   price

gàn ກັນ   each other

mŭan-gàn/kúu gàn ເໝືອນກັນ/ຄືກັນ   same, to look like

kâai-kúu-gàn ຄ້າຍຄືກັນ   to look like

tao-gàn/tao-găp ເທົ່າກັນ/ເທົ່າກັບ   equal

Other Helpful Nouns

nàa ໜ້າ   page

dtùa(dtòo)-nǎng-sǔu ຕົວ (ໂຕ) ໜັງສື   letter of the alphabet

dtuk-ga-dtàa ຕຸກກະຕາ   doll

yàa-sùup ຢາສູບ   cigarette

wáa-la-sǎan ວາລະສານ   magazine

mîit ມີດ   knife

tían ທຽນ   candle

kĕm ເຂັມ   needle

ka-nŏm-òm ຂະໜົມອົມ   candy

gêɛo/jɔ̀ɔk-gêɛo ແກ້ວ/ຈອກແກ້ວ   glass

jɔɔk ຈອກ	cup
màak-mâi ໝາກໄມ້	fruit
màak-gûai ໝາກກ້ວຍ	banana
màak-muang ໝາກມ່ວງ	mango
màak-hung ໝາກຮຸ່ງ	papaya
màak-gîang ໝາກກ້ຽງ	orange
màak-pâao ໝາກພ້າວ	coconut
màak-móo ໝາກໂມ	watermelon
dɔ̀ɔk-mâi ດອກໄມ້	flower
dɔ̀ɔk-gù-làap ດອກກຸຫລາບ	rose
jàan ຈານ	plate
gɛ̂ɛo ແກ້ວ	bottle
hìip/gǎp ຫີບ/ກັບ	box
kai ໄຂ່	egg
kào-pǎt/kùa-kào ເຂົ້າຜັດ/ຂົ້ວເຂົ້າ	fried rice
ga-dàan ກະດານ	board
maak-baan ໝາກບານ	ball
jǒt-mǎai ຈົດໝາຍ	letter
èek-ga-sǎan ເອກະສານ	document
dtûu-yèn ຕູ້ເຢັນ	refrigerator
kɔ́m-píu-dtɚ̀ɚ ຄອມພິວເຕີ	computer
buang ບ່ວງ	spoon
sɔm ສ້ອມ	fork
kán-hom ຄັນຮົ່ມ	umbrella
àa-káan/dtǔk ອາຄານ/ຕຶກ	building
kào-jii ເຂົ້າຈີ່	bread
sîin ຊີ້ນ	meat
ka-nǒm/kào nǒm ຂະໜົມ/ເຂົ້າໜົມ	cookie
sân ຊັ້ນ	floor, grade in school
sa-nit ຊະນິດ	kind (of things)

nâm-dtàan ນ້ຳຕານ	sugar
glɨa ເກືອ	salt
fiim ຟິມ	film
tep/ga-sɛt ເທັບ/ກະເຊັຶດ	casette tape
wíi-dìi-òo ວິດີໂອ	video
sa-dtɛm ສະແຕມ	stamp
dàao ດາວ	star
dtàa wén/dùang-àa-tit	sun
ຕາເວັນ/ດວງອາທິດ	
dùang-jan/pa-jàn/dɨan	moon
ດວງຈັນ/ພະຈັນ/ເດືອນ	
kɔ̌ɔng-kwǎn ຂອງຂວັນ	present
ta-nǒn ຖະໜົນ	road
táang-lot-fái ທາງລົດໄຟ	railway
kɔ̌ɔng/hɔng ຄອງ/ຮ່ອງ	canal
sǐi-nêe/hǔup-ngáo	movie
ຊີເນ່/ຮູບເງົາ	
lɨang ເລື້ອງ	story

lak-sǎ-na-náam ລັກສະນະນາມ Classifiers

Classifiers are words which are required in Lao when counting or referring to any concrete noun.

English has similar words. When we say "three glasses of water", "one sheet of paper", "eight head of cattle", the words "glasses", "sheet" and "head" could be called classifiers. Lao, however, uses classifiers much more often than English. It is impossible to speak acceptable Lao without mastering the use of classifiers.

A classifier is generally used with a category of nouns perceived to have a common characteristic. These categories often seem arbitrary. Therefore, it is a good idea to memorize the classifier along with the noun when learning new vocabulary.

Common Classifiers

1. kón (ຄົນ) » people.
2. dtùa/dtòo (ຕົວ/ໂຕ) » animals, tables, chairs, shirts, costumes,
   letters of the alphabet, dolls, cigarettes, etc.
3. lèm (ເຫຼັ້ມ) » candles, needles.
4. hŭa (ຫົວ) » books, notebooks, magazines.
5. àn (ອັນ) » pieces of candy, ashtrays, round objects,
   objects with unknown classifiers, stamps.
6. jɔ̀ɔk (ຈອກ) » glasses, cups, numbers of glasses of beer, cups
   of tea, coffe, water, etc.
7. pɛn (ແຜ່ນ) » boards, pieces of paper.
8. nuai (ໝ່ວຍ) » fruits, mountains, balls and other round things,
   radios, T.Vs., refrigerators, computers, electrical or
   mechanical machines, clocks, watches.
9. sa-băp (ສະບັບ) » newspapers, letters, documents.
10. lám (ລຳ) » ships, boats, airplanes.
11. kán (ຄັນ) » cars, motorcycles, bicycles, umbrellas, fishing
   rods.
12. gâan (ກ້ານ) » spoons, forks, pens.
13. lăng (ຫຼັງ) » houses, buildings.
14. gɔ̂ɔn (ກ້ອນ) » pieces of bread, pieces of meat, cookies,
   bars of soap, sugar cubes, pieces of candy, etc.
15. dtɔn (ຕ່ອນ) » pieces of meat.
16. chân (ຊັ້ນ) » floors of buildings, grades or classes in
   schools, classes of train or airplane seats.
17. hɔ̀ng (ຫ້ອງ) » rooms.
18. dɔ̀ɔk (ດອກ) » flowers.
19. kâng/tɯa (ຄັ້ງ/ເທື່ອ) » times (numbers of occurrences).
20. yàang (ຢ່າງ) » kinds of things, numbers of things.

21. bɔn (ບ່ອນ) » numbers of seats.

22. tùai (ຖ້ວຍ) » numbers of cups of soup, etc.

23. kùat (ຂວດ) » numbers of bottles of beer, water, etc.

24. jàan (ຈານ) » numbers of plates of rice, dishes, food, etc.

25. sèn (ເສັ້ນ) » threads, neckties, tires, necklaces,
         bracelets, roads, hairs, pieces of chalk, roads, railways.

26. gɔɔk (ກອກ) » cigarettes.

27. mûan (ມ້ວນ) » rolls of film, casette tapes, video tapes.

28. dùang (ດວງ) » stars, suns, moons, knives.

29. hɔɔ (ຫໍ່) » presents, bags of sweets, bags of snacks,
         wrapped things.

30. lám (ລຳ) » rivers, canals.

31. kuu (ຄູ່) » pairs of things or people.

32. sut (ຊຸດ) » sets of things, suits, dresses.

33. lɨang (ເລື່ອງ) » movies, plays, stories.

34. dtôn (ຕົ້ນ) » trees.

35. gɔɔ (ກໍ້) » rolls of film, small and round objects.

How to Use Classifiers

1. noun + cardinal number + <u>classifier</u>
   (one, two, three, ... nɯng, sɔ̌ɔng, sǎam)
   e.g. mǎa sǎam <u>dtòo</u> = three dogs
         kɔ̌i mɨ́i mǎa sǎam <u>dtòo</u>. = I have three dogs.
         bpɨ̂m hâa <u>hǔa</u> = five books
         bpɨ̂m hâa <u>hǔa</u> yùu tʉ́ng dtó.
              = Five books are on the table.

   nɯng is usually replaced with <u>dìao</u> (ฺฺฺฺฺฺฺฺฺฺ) in normal speech and
   <u>dìao</u> is placed after the classifier.
   e.g.   mǎa nɯng <u>dtòo</u> = mǎa <u>dtòo</u> dìao (one dog)

2. noun + <u>classifier</u> + nɨ́i, nán (*or* hàn) or pûun (*or* pûn)
   e.g. mǎa <u>dtòo</u> nɨ́i = this dog
        mǎa <u>dtòo</u> nɨ́i ngáam. = This dog is beautiful.
        bpɨ̂m <u>hǔa</u> nán = that book
        bpɨ̂m <u>hǔa</u> nán tao-dǎi? = How much is that book?

3. noun + <u>classifier</u> + ordinal number
   (first, second, third, ... (ที่) tîi nɯng, tîi sɔ̌ɔng, tîi sǎam)
   e.g. mǎa <u>dtòo</u> tîi nɯng = the first dog
        mǎa <u>dtòo</u> tîi nɯng sǐi dàm. = The first dog is black.
        bpɨ̂m <u>hǔa</u> tîi sɔ̌ɔng = the second book
        bpɨ̂m <u>hǔa</u> tîi sɔ̌ɔng yùu tʉ́ng dtó.
             = The second book is on the table.

   tîi nɯng is sometimes replaced with <u>lêɛk</u> (ฺฺฺฺฺ) or <u>tám-ìt</u> (ฺฺฺฺฺฺ) in
   normal speech.
   e.g.   bpɨ̂m <u>hǔa</u> tîi nɯng = bpɨ̂m <u>hǔa</u> lêɛk (the first book)

4. noun + jǎk + classifier
    (asking for the number or amount of something)
        e.g. mǎa jǎk dtòo? = how many dogs?
             jâo mîi mǎa jǎk dtòo.
             = How many dogs do you have?
             bpȗm jǎk hǔa. = how many books?
             láao aan bpȗm jǎk hǔa.
             = How many books did he read?

5. ˙noun + classifier + adjective
        e.g. mǎa dtòo mai = a new dog
             kɔ̌i mîi mǎa dtòo mai. = I have a new dog.
             bpȗm hǔa gao = an old book
             nîi mɛɛn bpȗm hǔa gao. = This is an old book.

6. noun + classifier + dǎi = which one.
        e.g. mǎa dtòo dǎi. = Which dog?
             jâo mak mǎa dtòo dǎi tîi sùt.
             = Which dog do you like most?
             bpȗm hǔa dǎi. = Which book?
             bpȗm hǔa dǎi kɔ̌ɔng jâo.
             = Which one is your book?

7. (noun) + lǎai (ຫລາຍ) + classifier = many _____
        e.g. mǎa lǎai dtòo or lǎai dtòo = many dogs

Note: When a noun is understood from the context, it is often omitted.
        e.g.   hàa hǔa = five books
               hǔa nîi = this book
               hǔa lêɛk = the first book
               jǎk hǔa = how many books?
               hǔa gao = an old book
               hǔa dǎi = which book?

Conversation

John: ga-bpǎo nuai nân láa-káa tao-dǎi.

ຈອມ: ກະເປົ໋າ   ໜ່ວຍ   ນັ້ນ   ລາຄາ   ເທົ່າໃດ?

Konkǎai-kuang: hàa hɔ̂ɔi gìip.

ຄົນຂາຍເຄື່ອງ: ຫ້າ   ຮ້ອຍ   ກີບ.

It's five hundred kip.

John: nuai nîi děe.

ຈອມ: ໜ່ວຍ   ນີ້   ເດ?

What about this one?

Konkǎai-kuang: àn-nân sǎam hɔ̂ɔi hàa sǐp.

ຄົນຂາຍເຄື່ອງ: ອັນນັ້ນ   ສາມ   ຮ້ອຍ   ຫ້າ   ສິບ.

That one is three hundred and fifty.

John: jâo míi jǎk sǐi.

ຈອມ: ເຈົ້າ   ມີ   ຈັກ   ສີ?   ↖

How many colors do you have?

Konkǎai-kuang: míi lǎai sǐi.

ຄົນຂາຍເຄື່ອງ: ມີ   ຫລາຍ   ສີ.

Many colors.

jâo mak sǐi nyǎng lǎai tii-sǔt.

ເຈົ້າ   ມັກ   ສີ   ຫຍັງ   ຫລາຍ   ທີ່ສຸດ?

What color do you like the most?

John: kɔ̀i mak sǐi dàm lǎai tii sǔt.

ຈອມ: ຂ້ອຍ   ມັກ   ສີ   ດໍາ   ຫລາຍ   ທີ່   ສຸດ.

I like black the most.

kɔ̀i kɔ̌ɔ bəng nuai sǐi dàm gǎp sǐi kàao nân dɛɛ.

ຂ້ອຍ   ຂໍ   ເບິ່ງ   ໜ່ວຍ   ສີ   ດໍາ   ກັບ   ສີ   ຂາວ   ນັ້ນ   ແດ່?

May I see the black and the white ones?

Konkǎai-kʉang: nîi dee*.

ຄົນຂາຍເຄື່ອງ: ນີ້ ເດ.

      Here you are.

John: kɔ̀i kit waa kɔ̀i mak nuai sǐi dàm lǎai gwaa.

ຈອນ: ຂ້ອຍ ຄິດ ວ່າ ຂ້ອຍ ມັກ ໜ່ວຍ ສີ ດຳ ຫລາຍ ກວ່າ.

      I think I like black better.

      láa-káa tao-dǎi gǒ.

      ລາຄາ   ເທົ່າໃດ ກໍ?

      How much is it again?

Konkǎai-kʉang: hàa hɔ̌ɔi.

ຄົນຂາຍເຄື່ອງ: ຫ້າ ຮ້ອຍ.

      Five hundred.

John: sii hɔ̌ɔi dâi bɔɔ

ຈອນ: ສີ່ ຮ້ອຍ ໄດ້ ບໍ?

      Can you make it four hundred?

Konkǎai: bɔɔ dâi dɔ̌ɔk*. ào sii hɔ̌ɔi hàa sǐp sǎa*.

ຄົນຂາຍເຄື່ອງ: ບໍ່ ໄດ້ ດອກ.   ເອົາ ສີ່ ຮ້ອຍ ຫ້າ ສິບ ຊ່າ.

      No, I can't. Let's make it four hundred and fifty.

John: dtǒk-lóng.

ຈອນ: ຕົກລົງ.

*ending particles used for emphasis

bpà-nyòok   ปะโทยภ   **Sentences**

1. A: láao sǔung gwàa kɔ̀i.

   ลาว ສູງ ກວ່າ ຂ້ອຍ.

   He is taller than I.

   B: bpûm hǔa nîi péeng gwaa hǔa nân.

   ປຶ້ມ ຫົວ ນີ້ ແພງ ກວ່າ ຫົວ ນັ້ນ.

   This book is more expensive than that one.

   C: hǔa nîi dìi gwaa.

   ຫົວ ນີ້ ດິ ກວ່າ.

   This one is better.

   D: hǔa nân ngáam gwaa.

   ຫົວ ນັ້ນ ງາມ ກວ່າ.

   That one is more beautiful.

2. A: láao sǔung tii-sǔt nái hɔ̀ng.

   ລາວ ສູງ ທີ່ສຸດ ໃນ ຫ້ອງ.

   He is the tallest in the room.

   B: bpûm hǔa nîi péeng tii-sǔt.

   ປຶ້ມ ຫົວ ນີ້ ແພງ ທີ່ສຸດ.

   This book is the most expensive.

   C: àn-nîi dìi tii-sǔt.

   ອັນນີ້ ດິ ທີ່ ສຸດ.

   This is the best.

   D: àn-nân ngáam tii-sǔt.

   ອັນນັ້ນ ງາມ ທີ່ສຸດ.

   That one is the most beautiful.

3. A: láao gǎp jâo mɛɛn* pǎi sǔung gwaa gàn.

   ລາວ ກັບ ເຈົ້າ ແມ່ນ ໃຜ ສູງ ກວ່າ ກັນ?

   Who is taller between him and you?

   *mɛɛn is often used in front of question words for emphasis.

B: láao sŭung gwaa (kɔ̀i).

ลาວ   สูງ ກວ່າ (ຂ້ອຍ).

He is taller (than I).

A: bpûm hŭa nîi gǎp hŭa nân,

ປຶ້ມ   ຫົວ ນີ້ ກັບ ຫົວ ນັ້ນ,

àn dǎi péɛng gwaa gàn.

ອັນ ໃດ ແພງ ກວ່າ ກັນ?

Between this book and that book,

which one is more expensive?

B: bpûm hŭa nîi péɛng gwaa (hŭa nân).

ປຶ້ມ   ຫົວ ນີ້ ແພງ ກວ່າ (ຫົວ ນັ້ນ).

This book is more expensive (than that one).

A: àn-dǎi dìi gwaa.

ອັນໃດ   ດີ ກວ່າ?

Which one is better?

B: àn-nîi dìi gwaa.

ອັນນີ້ ດີ ກວ່າ.

This one is better.

A: àn-dǎi ngáam gwaa.

ອັນໃດ   ງາມ ກວ່າ?

Which one is more beautiful?

B: àn-nân ngáam gwaa.

ອັນນັ້ນ ງາມ ກວ່າ.

That one is more beautiful.

4. A: A nyai gwaa B, dtɛɛ C nyai tii-sǔt.

A ໃຫຍ່ ກວ່າ B,   ແຕ່ C ໃຫຍ່ ທີ່ສຸດ.

A is bigger than B, but C is the biggest.

B: kɔ̀i mak sǐi kǎao lǎai gwaa sǐi dàm,

ຂ້ອຍ ມັກ ສີ ຂາວ ຫລາຍ ກວ່າ ສີ ດຳ.

dtɛɛ kɔ̀i mak sǐi fâa lǎai tii sǔt.

ແຕ່ ຂ້ອຍ ມັກ ສີ ຟ້າ ຫລາຍ ທີ່ສຸດ.

I like white more than black, but I like blue the most.

5. A: húa-bìn lám nîi nyai tii-sǔt nái lôok.
       ເຮືອບິນ ລຳ ນີ້ ໃຫຍ່ ທີ່ສຸດ ໃນ ໂລກ.
       This airplane is the biggest in the world.

    B: kɔ̀i sǔung tii-sǔt nái hǔan.
       ຂ້ອຍ ສູງ ທີ່ສຸດ ໃນ ເຮືອນ.
       I am the tallest in the house.

    C: láao hang-míi tii-sǔt nái mɯ́ang-láao.
       ລາວ ຮັ່ງມີ ທີ່ສຸດ ໃນ ເມືອງລາວ.
       He is the richest in Laos.

6. A: àn-nîi gǎp àn-nân kɯ́ɯ-gàn.
       ອັນນີ້ ກັບ ອັນນັ້ນ ຄືກັນ.
       This one and that one are the same.
       (Literally: This one and that one look like each other.)

    B: sɔ̌ɔng kón nân bəng kâai-kɯ́ɯ-gàn.
       ສອງ ຄົນ ນັ້ນ ເບິ່ງ ຄ້າຍຄືກັນ.
       Those two people look alike.

    C: bpɯ̂m sɔ̌ɔng hǔa nîi láa-káa tao-gàn.
       ປຶ້ມ ສອງ ຫົວ ນີ້ ລາຄາ ເທົ່າກັນ.
       The price of these two books is the same.

7.   kǎo-jâo hak gàn lǎai.
       ເຂົາເຈົ້າ ຮັກ ກັນ ຫລາຍ.
       They love each other very much.

8.   láao sáng jâo nyɔ̂ɔn waa jâo mak kìi-dtǔa.
       ລາວ ຊັ່ງ ເຈົ້າ ຍ້ອນ ວ່າ ເຈົ້າ ມັກ ຂີ້ຕົວະ.
       He hates you because you often lie.
       (Literally: ... because you like to lie.)

9. A: hǔan jâo míi sǎt-líang bɔɔ?
       ເຮືອນ ເຈົ້າ ມີ ສັດລ້ຽງ ບໍ່?
       Do you have pets at home?

    B: míi. míi mɛ́ɛo sɔ̌ɔng dtòo.
       ມີ. ມີ ແມວ ສອງ ໂຕ.
       Yes. I have two cats.

The following sentences demonstrate how to use different classifiers. The underlined words are classifiers.

10.   míi kón hàa <u>kón</u> yuu nái hòng.

ມີ   ຄົນ   ຫ້າ   ຄົນ   ຢູ່ ໃນ ຫ້ອງ.

There are five people in the room.

11.   sùa <u>dtòo</u> nîi bɔɔ péɛng.

ເສື້ອ ໂຕ   ນີ້   ບໍ່ ແພງ.

This shirt is not expensive.

12.   pǎi kǐan bpûm <u>hǔa</u> nân.

ໃຜ ຂຽນ   ປຶ້ມ   ຫົວ   ນັ້ນ?

Who wrote that book?

13.   jâo mak <u>àn</u> dǎi lǎai tii-sǔt.

ເຈົ້າ   ມັກ   ອັນ   ໃດ ຫລາຍ ທີ່ສຸດ?

Which one do you like the best?

14.   hìip <u>nuai</u> nîi bɔɔ kɔi dìi.

ຫີບ ຫນ່ວຍ   ນີ້   ບໍ່ ຄ່ອຍ ດີ.

This bag is not very good.

15.   jîa <u>pɛn</u> nân bàang lǎai.

ເຈ້ຍ ແຜ່ນ ນັ້ນ   ບາງ   ຫລາຍ.

This piece of paper is very thin.

16.   mûu-nîi kɔ̀i gìn màak-gûai sɔ̌ong <u>nuai</u>.

ມື້ນີ້   ຂ້ອຍ   ກິນ   ຫມາກກ້ວຍ   ສອງ ຫນ່ວຍ.

Today I ate two bananas.

17.   mûu-wáan-nîi jâo aan nǎngsǔu-pím jak <u>sa-bǎp</u>.

ມື້ວານນີ້   ເຈົ້າ   ອ່ານ   ຫນັງສືພິມ   ຈັກ ສະບັບ?

How many newspapers did you read yesterday?

18.   kɔ̌i míi tóo-la-tat sǎam <u>nuai</u>, kɔ́mpíu-dtɚ̀ə <u>nuai</u> nɯng.

ຂ້ອຍ ມີ   ໂທລະທັດ   ສາມ   ຫນ່ວຍ,   ຄອມພິວເຕີ   ຫນ່ວຍ ຫນຶ່ງ.

I have three televisions and one computer.

19.   húa-bìn <u>lám</u> nîi máa jàak wíang-jàn.

ເຮືອບິນ   ລຳ   ນີ້   ມາ   ຈາກ   ວຽງຈັນ.

This airplane came from Vientiane.

20.   lot <u>kán</u> nîi het jàak yii-bpun.

ລົດ   ຄັນ   ນີ້ ເຣັດ   ຈາກ   ຍີ່ປຸ່ນ.

This car is made in Japan.

21.   kɔ̀i sɨ̂ɨ hɨ́an <u>lǎng</u> mai.

ຂ້ອຍ ຊື້ ເຮືອນ   ຫລັງ ໃໝ່.

I bought a new house.

22.   sîin nûa <u>dtɔn</u> nîi sɛ̂ɛp ii-lǐi.

ຊີ້ນ   ງົວ   ຕ່ອນ   ນີ້ ແຊບ   ອີຫລີ.

This piece of meat is really delicious.

23.   kɔ̀i yuu <u>sân</u> tii sǎam.

ຂ້ອຍ ຢູ່   ຊັ້ນ ທີ   ສາມ.

I live on the third floor.

24.   hɨ́an láao míi hɔ̀ng-nɔ́ɔn sii <u>hɔ̀ng</u>.

ເຮືອນ ລາວ   ມີ   ຫ້ອງນອນ ສີ່ ຫ້ອງ.

His house has four bedrooms.

25.   dɔ̀ɔk-mâi <u>dɔ̀ɔk</u> nîi ngáam lǎai.

ດອກໄມ້   ດອກ   ນີ້ ງາມ   ຫລາຍ.

This flower is very beautiful.

26.   kɔ̀i kɤ́əi bpài mɨ́ang láao hàa <u>tɨa</u>.

ຂ້ອຍ ເຄີຍ ໄປ   ເມືອງ ລາວ   ຫ້າ ເທື່ອ.

I have been to Laos five times.

27.   yuu táng dto míi àa-hǎan hŏk <u>yɨang</u> .

ຢູ່ ເທິງ ໂຕະ ມີ   ອາຫານ   ຫົກ ຍື່ອງ .

There are five kinds of food on the table.

28.   kɔ̌ɔ kào nɨng <u>jàan</u>.

ຂໍ ເຂົ້າ ໝຶ່ງ ຈານ.

Give me one (plate of) rice.

29.   kɔ̌ɔ nâm yèn sɔ̌ɔng <u>jɔ̀ɔk</u>.

ຂໍ ນ້ຳ ເຢັນ ສອງ ຈອກ.

Give me two glasses of cold water.

30. kɔ̌ɔ gàa-fée hɔ̂ɔn sǎam <u>jɔ̀ɔk</u>.

ຂໍ   ກາເຟ   ຮ້ອນ   ສາມ   <u>ຈອກ</u>.

Give me three cups of hot coffee.

31. ào bìa   sii   <u>gɛ́ɛo</u>.

ເອົາ ເບຍ   ສີ່   <u>ແກ້ວ</u>.

I want four bottles of beer.

32. ào kâo-pǎt hàa <u>jàan</u>.

ເອົາ ເຂົ້າຜັດ ຫ້າ   <u>ຈານ</u>.

I want five plates of fried rice.

33. ào nâm-dtàan hǒk <u>gɔ̂ɔn</u>.

ເອົາ   ນ້ຳຕານ   ຫົກ   <u>ກ້ອນ</u>.

I want six cubes of sugar.

34. A: jâo míi bpàak-gàa jǎk <u>gâan</u>.

ເຈົ້າ ມີ   ປາກກາ   ຈັກ <u>ກ້ານ</u>?

How many pens do you have?

B: míi sɔ̌ɔng <u>gâan</u>.

ມີ   ສອງ   <u>ກ້ານ</u>.

I have two.

A: jâo míi sɔ̌ɔ jǎk <u>sèn</u>.

ເຈົ້າ ມີ   ສໍ   ຈັກ <u>ເສັ້ນ</u>?

How many pencils do you have?

B: míi sèn dìao.

ມີ <u>ເສັ້ນ</u> ດຽວ.

I have one.

35. sɔ̀i <u>sèn</u> nîi láa-káa tâo-dǎi.

ສ້ອຍ <u>ເສັ້ນ</u> ນີ້   ລາຄາ ເທົ່າໃດ?

How much is this necklace?

36. láao sùup-yàa mǔu la sǐp <u>gɔ̀ɔk</u>.

ລາວ   ສູບຢາ   ມື້   ລະ ສິບ <u>ກອກ</u>.

He smokes ten cigarettes a day.

37.   pûak-háo gàmláng bəng wíi-dìi-òo <u>mûan</u> tii săam yuu.

ພວກເຮົາ ກຳລັງ ເບິ່ງ ວິດີໂອ <u>ມ້ວນ</u> ທີ່ ສາມ ຢູ່.

We are watching the third video.

38.   kɔ̀i sɨ̂ɨ sa-dtɛ̀m sáao <u>àn</u>.

ຂ້ອຍ ຊື້ ສະແຕມ ຊາວ <u>ອັນ</u>.

I bought twenty stamps.

39.   láao dâi móong <u>nuai</u> mai.

ລາວ ໄດ້ ໂມງ <u>ໜ່ວຍ</u> ໃໝ່.

He has a new watch.

40.   mɛɛ sɨ̂ɨ kào-nŏm sii <u>hɔɔ</u>.

ແມ່ ຊື້ ເຂົ້າໜົມ ສີ່ <u>ຫໍ່</u>.

Mother bought four packages of snacks.

41.   mɛɛ-nâm <u>lám</u> nîi yáao lăai.

ແມ່ນ້ຳ <u>ລຳ</u> ນີ້ ຍາວ ຫລາຍ.

This river is very long.

42.   gə̀əp <u>kuu</u> nân ngáam tii-sŭt.

ເກີບ <u>ຄູ່</u> ນັ້ນ ງາມ ທີ່ສຸດ.

That pair of shoes is the prettiest.

43.   bpɨ̂m <u>sut</u> nîi bpèn-dtàa-sŏn-jài.

ປຶ້ມ <u>ຊຸດ</u> ນີ້ ເປັນຕາສົນໃຈ.

This set of books is interesting.

44.   kɨ́ɨn-wáan-nîi kɔ̀i bəng hûup-ngáo săam <u>luang</u>.

ຄືນວານນີ້ ຂ້ອຍ ເບິ່ງ ຮູບເງົາ ສາມ <u>ເລື້ອງ</u>.

Last night I watched three movies.

45.   dtôn mâi <u>dtôn</u> nân àa-nyu lăai gwàa pán bpìi.

ຕົ້ນໄມ້ <u>ຕົ້ນ</u> ນັ້ນ ອາຍຸ ຫລາຍ ກວ່າ ພັນ ປີ.

That tree is more than a thousand years old.

Test 10

Matching

A   Adjectives

____ 1. tall
____ 2. new
____ 3. fat
____ 4. cold
____ 5. intelligent
____ 6. small
____ 7. far
____ 8. busy
____ 9. rich
____ 10. special

a. nɔ̌ɔi   ນ້ອຍ
b. gài   ໄກ
c. sǔung   ສູງ
d. nǎk   ໜັກ
e. nǎao   ໜາວ
f. nyùng   ຫຍຸ້ງ
g. pi-sèet   ພິເສດ
h. hang-míi   ຣັ່ງມີ
i. dtùi   ຕຸ້ຍ
j. gâi   ໃກ້
k. sa-làat   ສະຫລາດ
l. mai   ໃໝ່
m. tuk/jòn   ທຸກ/ຈົນ

B   Nouns

____ 1. cigarette
____ 2. magazine
____ 3. letter
____ 4. meat
____ 5. plate
____ 6. sugar
____ 7. movie
____ 8. story

____ 9. building
____ 10. star

a. hûup-ngáo   ຮູບເງົາ
b. kùat   ຂວດ
c. jàan   ຈານ
d. sîin   ຊີ້ນ
e. jǒt-mǎai   ຈົດໝາຍ
f. àa-káan/dtǔk   ອາຄານ/ຕຶກ
g. dàao   ດາວ
h. wáa-la-sǎan
      ວາລະສານ
i. gùa   ເກືອ
j. lɨang   ເລື້ອງ
k. yàa-sùup   ຢາສູບ
l. buang   ບ່ວງ
m. nâam-dtàan   ນ້ຳຕານ

C   Classifiers

Match the following nouns with their proper classifiers.

_____ 1. mǎa   ໝາ   a. kùat   ขวด

_____ 2. lot-yón   ລົດຍົນ   b. tɛng   ແທ່ງ

_____ 3. nǎng-sǔu-pím   ໜັງສືພິມ   c. gâan   ກ້ານ

_____ 4. hǔa-bìn   ເຮືອບິນ   d. kán   ຄັນ

_____ 5. bìa   ເບຍ   e. nuai   ໝ່ວຍ

_____ 6. hǔan   ເຮືອນ   f. sèn   ເສັ້ນ

_____ 7. tíi-wíi   ທີວີ   g. dtùa   ໂຕ

_____ 8. sɔ̌ɔ-dàm   ສໍດຳ   h. lám   ລຳ

_____ 9. jîa   ເຈ້ຍ   j. sa-bǎp   ສະບັບ

_____ 10. ta-nǒn   ຖະໜົນ   k. pɛn/bài   ແຜ່ນ/ໃບ

                                       l. lǎng   ຫຼັງ

                                       m. àn   ອັນ

Translate the following into English.

1. A: màak-muang nuai   dǎi sêɛp tii-sǔt.
   ໝາກໝ່ວງ   ໜ່ວຍ   ໃດ ແຊບ ທີ່ສຸດ?

   B: kit waa nuai nîi sêɛp tii-sǔt.
   ຄິດ ວ່າ ໜ່ວຍ ນີ້ ແຊບ ທີ່ສຸດ.

---

2. A: hǔan jâo míi jǎk sân.   B: míi sǎam sân.
   ເຮືອນ ເຈົ້າ ມີ ຈັກ ຊັ້ນ?   ມີ ສາມ ຊັ້ນ.

---

3. A: hǔa lám lɛ̂ɛk jà máa mɯa-dǎi.
   ເຮືອ ລຳ ແລກ ຈະ ມາ ເມື່ອໃດ?

   B: jà máa mɯ̂ɯ-ɯɯn.
   ຈະ ມາ ມື້ອື່ນ.

---

4. mɯ́ɯ-wáan-níi sɯ̂ɯ moóng hɯan mai.
   ເມື່ອວານນີ້ ຊື້ ໂມງ ເຮືອນ ໃໝ່.

---

5. tii sǔan-sǎt míi sâang hǎa dtoo.
   ທີ່ ສວນສັຕວ໌ ມີ ຊ້າງ ຫ້າ ໂຕ.

Reading Exercise

Read the following sentences aloud and translate.

1. ອາເມລິກາ ໃຫຍ່ ກວ່າ ເມືອງ ລາວ .

2. ລົດ ຄັນ ນັ້ນ ງາມ ທີ່ສຸດ .

3. ຂ້ອຍ ມັກ ສີ ຂາວ ຫລາຍ ກວ່າ ສີ ດຳ .

4. ລາວ ມີ ໝາ ສາມ ໂຕ .

5. ລູກຊາຍ ຂ້ອຍ ຍາກ ເປັນ ນັກບິນ .

6. ເຈົ້າ ມີ ພີ່ນ້ອງ ຈັກ ຄົນ?

7. ເອື້ອຍ ເຈົ້າ ເຮັດ ວຽກ ຫຍັງ?

8. ເປັນຫຍັງ ຄົນ ຍີ່ປຸ່ນ ຈິ່ງ ມັກ ເຮັດ ວຽກ?

9. ຂ້ອຍ ຍາກ ຈະ ມີ ລູກ ສອງ ຄົນ .

10. ມື້ວານນີ້ ຂ້ອຍ ຊື້ ເກີບ ສອງ ຄູ່ .

11. ທ້າວ ສອນ ເວົ້າ ພາສາ ອັງກິດ ບໍ່ ຄ່ອຍ ຖືກ .

12. ເປັນຫຍັງ ເຈົ້າ ຈິ່ງ ບໍ່ ໄປ ເຮັດ ວຽກ?

13. ເຈົ້າ ອາຍຸ ເທົ່າໃດ?

14. ຂ້ອຍ ເປັນ ນັກທຸລະກິດ .

15. ລາວ ມີ ຄົນຮັກ ຫລາຍ ຄົນ .

16. ຂ້ອຍ ກຳລັງ ແຕ່ງໂຕ .

17. ຂ້ອຍ ຊັກ ເຄື່ອງນຸ່ງ ທຸກມື້.

18. ມື້ອື່ນ ຂ້ອຍ ຈະ ໄປ ຕັດ ຜົມ.

19. ຂ້ອຍ ມີ ວຽກ ຫລາຍ ອິຫລີ.

20. ຖ້າ ເຈົ້າ ມີ ເງິນ ຫລາຍໆ ເຈົ້າ ຈະ ເຮັດ ຫຍັງ?

21. ມື້ນີ້ ຂ້ອຍ ບໍ່ ຄ່ອຍ ສະບາຍ.

22. ມື້ອື່ນ ຂ້ອຍ ໄປ ຫລິ້ນ ບໍ່ ໄດ້.

23. ຮຽນ ພາສາ ລາວ ມ່ວນ ຫລາຍ.

24. ຜູ້ຊາຍ ຄົນ ນັ້ນ ມັກ ອ່ານ ຫນັງສື.

25. ຫ້ອງນ້ຳ ຜູ້ຍິງ ຢູ່ໃສ?

26. ທ່ານ ຄຳ ຢູ່ ຫ້ອງ ສອງ.

27. ຂ້ອຍ ມັກ ອ່ານ ຫນັງສືພິມ ພາສາ ອັງກິດ.

28. ຄູວນີ້ ລາວ ບໍ່ຄ່ອຍ ໄປ ຮຽນ ພາສາລາວ ຢູ່ ວັດ.

29. ຮ້ານອາຫານ ຢູ່ໃກ້ ກັບ ໂຮງແຮມ ວັງວຽງ.

30. ຂ້ອຍ ຢາກ ເຂົ້າ ຫລາຍ ເພາະວ່າ ຂ້ອຍ ບໍ່ ໄດ້ ກິນ ເຂົ້າເຊົ້າ.

31. ເປັນຫຍັງ ຄົນນັ້ນ ຈິ່ງ ບໍ່ ຢາກ ໄປທ່ຽວ ກັບ ເຮົາ.

32. ລາວ ບອກວ່າ ກິນ ບໍ່ ໄດ້ ເພາະວ່າ ມັນ ເຜັດ ຫລາຍໂພດ.

33. ນ້ອງຊາຍ ຂ້ອຍ ບໍ່ມັກ ອ່ານ ໜັງສືພິມ ແຕ່ ລາວ ມັກ ເບິ່ງ ໂທລະພາບ.

34. ລາວ ເປັນ ມັກ ຫຸລະກິດ ທີ່ ເກາະ ອິຫລີ.

35. ເຮືອນ ຫລັງ ນີ້ ກັບ ຫລັງ ນັ້ນ ຫລັງ ໃດ ງາມ ກວ່າກັນ.

36. ເຮືອນ ເຈົ້າ ມີ ສັດລັງ ບໍ່?

37. ເຮົາ ຂາຍ ອາຫານ ຢູ່ທີ່ ເມືອງ ແອລເອ ອາເມລິກາ.

38. ອາທິດ ທີ່ແລ້ວ ເຮົາ ໄປ ຫລິ້ນ ສວນສັດ.

39. ຄອບຄົວ ຂອງ ຂ້ອຍ ມີ ຫ້າ ຄົນ.

40. ທ່ານ ພອນ ເປັນ ພະນັກງານລັດ ທີ່ ເມືອງ ລາວ.

Read the following paragraphs aloud and translate.

ຄອບຄົວຂອງຂ້ອຍແມ່ນຄອບຄົວໃຫຍ່. ໃນເຮືອນຂ້ອຍມີທັງໝົດ ແປດຄົນ. ມີພໍ່, ແມ່, ເອື້ອຍ 2 ຄົນ, ອ້າຍ 1 ຄົນ, ນ້ອຍຊາຍ 1 ຄົນ, ນ້ອງສາວ 1 ຄົນ ແລະໂຕຂ້ອຍ. ພໍ່ຂອງ ຂ້ອຍເປັນຊາວນາ. ແມ່ຂອງຂ້ອຍເປັນແມ່ເຮືອນ. ພວກເຮົາບໍ່ມີ ເງິນຫລາຍ ແຕ່ກໍເປັນຄອບຄົວທີ່ມີຄວາມສຸກ.

ມື້ວານນີ້ຂ້ອຍໄປຊື້ເຄື່ອງຢູ່ທີ່ຕະຫລາດເຊົ້າ. ຊື້ກຶບມາ ຄູ່ນຶ່ງ, ທຶບສອງໜ່ວຍ, ປຶ້ມສາມຫົວ, ປາກກາສີ້ຫ້ານ, ແລະສໍຄຳ ຫ້າຫ້ານ.

ໝູ່ສະໜິດຄົນນຶ່ງຂອງຂ້ອຍຊື່ລໍາແພງ. ລາວອາໄສຢູ່ເມືອງ ຫລວງພະບາງ. ແຕ່ທ່ອນລາວຢູ່ເມືອງວຽງຈັນເຊິ່ມກ່ຽວກັບ ຂ້ອຍ. ພວກເຮົາເຄີຍໄປໂຮງຮຽນນຳກັນ. ຂ້ອຍບໍ່ໄດ້ພົບກັບ ລາວຫລາຍປີແລ້ວ, ແຕ່ພວກເຮົາຕຳຕິດຕໍ່ກັນທາງຈົດໝາຍ ຢູ່ສະເໝີ.

ນ້ອຍເປັນນັກສຶກສາຢູ່ທີ່ມະຫາວິທະຍາໄລ. ລາວກຳລັງຮຽນວິຊາ ພາສາອັງກິດເປັນວິຊາເອກ. ປີໜ້າລາວປາກຈະມາຮຽນ ທີ່ອາເມລິກາ. ລາວມີອ້າຍເຣ້ດວຽກຢູ່ທີ່ແອລເອ.

ເມືອງລາວມີອາຫານທີ່ແຊບຫລາຍຢ່າງ. ຕົວຢ່າງເຊັ່ນ, ລາບ, ຕຳໝາກຫຸ່ງ, ຕົ້ມປາລາວ, ມີ້ງປາ. ອາຫານລາວອາດເຜັດ ແຕ່ສຳລັບຊາວຕ່າງຊາດ, ແຕ່ຖ້າລິ້ງກັບບລິດຊາດທີ່ເຜັດແລ້ວ ຈະຮູ້ວ່າອາຫານລາວແຊບຫລາຍ.

ຄົນລາວເປັນຄົນຊາດທີ່ມັກຄວາມມ່ວນຊື່ນ. ຄົນມັກມາໂຮມກັນ ແລ້ວຈັດງານບຸນຕ່າງໆ. ມີການກິນອາຫານ, ຮ້ອງລຳ ທຳເພງ. ບໍ່ວ່າຄົນລາວຢູ່ບ່ອນໃດກໍຈະເອົາວັດທະນະທຳ, ປະເພນີຂອງຕົນໄປນຳ.

ຕອນນີ້ຄອບຄົວຂອງຂ້ອຍອາໄສຢູ່ໃນອາເມລິກາ. ພວກເຮົາຍ້າຍ ມາຢູ່ນີ້ໄດ້ເກືອບຂາວປີແລ້ວ. ກ່ອນມາຢູ່ປະເທດນີ້, ພວກເຮົາຢູ່ ສູນສຳລັບຜູ້ລົບພະຍົບທີ່ເມືອງໄທເປັນເວລາສາມປີ. ພວກເຮົາ ມັກແລະຮັກອາເມລິກາລິປະເທດຂອງຕົນເອງ.

Appendix I
Useful Words and Phrases

General Conversation

◆ Good morning. Good afternoon.   sa-bàai-dìi. ສະບາຍດີ.
   Good evening. Hello.

◆ How are you?   sa-bàai-dìi bɔɔ. ສະບາຍດີບໍ່?

◆ Fine.   sa-bàai-dìi. ສະບາຍດີ.

◆ Not so good.   bɔɔ kɔi sa-bàai. ບໍ່ຄ່ອຍສະບາຍ.

◆ See you tomorrow.   mûn ʉʉn pɔ̂ɔ gàn mai.
   ມື້ອື່ນພົ້ກັນໃໝ່.

◆ See you later.   lɛ̂ɛo pɔ̂ɔ gàn mai. ແລ້ວພົ້ກັນໃໝ່.

◆ Take care.   hak-sǎa dtùa-eeng dɛɛ dɔ̀ə.
   ຮັກສາຕົວເອງແດ່ດີ.

◆ Thank you.   kɔ̀ɔp-jài. ຂອບໃຈ.

◆ Never mind./ You're welcome.   bɔɔ bpèn nyǎng. ບໍ່ເປັນຫຍັງ.

◆ Excuse me./ I'm sorry.   kɔ̌ɔ-tôot. ຂໍໂທດ.

◆ Nice to meet you.   nyín-dìi tii dâi pop jâo.
   ຍິນດີທີ່ໄດ້ພົບເຈົ້າ.

◆ How have you been doing?   jâo sa-bàai dìi yuu bɔɔ.
   ເຈົ້າສະບາຍດີຢູ່ບໍ່?

◆ Long time no see.   bɔɔ dâi pop gàn dòn lɛ̂ɛo dée.
   ບໍ່ໄດ້ພົບກັນດົນແລ້ວເດ.

◆ This.   àn-nîi. ອັນນີ້.

◆ What's this?   àn-nii mɛɛn nyǎng.
   ອັນນີ້ແມ່ນຫຍັງ?

◆ That.   àn-nân. ອັນນັ້ນ.

◆ What's that?   àn-nân mɛɛn nyǎng.
   ອັນນັ້ນແມ່ນຫຍັງ?

◆ Here.   yuu nîi. ຢູ່ນີ້/ຢູ່ນີ້.

◆ There.   yuu nân. ຢູ່ນັ້ນ.

◆ What?   nyăng. ຫຍັງ?

◆ Who?   păi. ໃຜ?

◆ Whose?   kɔ̌ɔng-păi. ຂອງໃຜ?

◆ Where?   yuu-săi. ຢູ່ໃສ?

◆ When?   mɯa-dăi. ເມື່ອໃດ?

◆ Why?   bpèn-nyăng. ເປັນຫຍັງ?

◆ How?   yaang-dăi/jang-dăi.
                                    ຢ່າງໃດ/ຈັ່ງໃດ?

◆ How much?   tao-dăi. ເທົ່າໃດ?

◆ How much is this?   àn nîi láa-káa tao-dăi.
                                    ອັນນີ້ລາຄາເທົ່າໃດ?

◆ Hello (on the phone).   aa-lŏo. ອາໂຫລ.

◆ I'd like to speak (on the   kɔ̀i kɔ̌ɔ wâo găp _____ dɛɛ.
    phone) with _____.   ຂ້ອຍຂໍເວົ້າກັບ_____ ແດ່.

◆ Really?   mɛɛn tɛ̂ɛ bɔɔ. ແມ່ນແທ້ບໍ່?

◆ Yes.   mɛɛn. ແມ່ນ.

◆ No.   bɔɔ mɛɛn. ບໍ່ແມ່ນ.

◆ If.   tàa. ຖ້າ.

◆ Not yet.   nyáng tɯa. ຍັງເທື່ອ

◆ Already.   lɛ̂ɛo. ແລ້ວ.

◆ But.   dtɛɛ. ແຕ່.

◆ Because.   pɔ-waa/yɔ̌ɔn-waa.
                                    ເພາະວ່າ/ຍ້ອມວ່າ.

◆ Don't.   yaa. ຢ່າ.

◆ Don't do it.   yaa het. ຢ່າເຮັດ.

◆ O.K.   òo-kée. ໂອເຄ.

◆ So-so   jang sân là. ຈັ່ງຊັ້ນລະ.

◆ Maybe   bàang-tíi. ບາງທີ.

◆ Please   ga-lu-náa. ກະລຸນາ.

◆ Where are you going?   jâo si bpài săi. ເຈົ້າຊິໄປໃສ?

◆ Where have you been?   jâo bpài săi máa. ເຈົ້າໄປໃສມາ?

◆ Have you eaten?   gìn kào lέεo bɔɔ. ກິນເຂົ້າແລ້ວບໍ່?

◆ How's business?   tu-la-gĭt bpèn jang dăi.
                 ທຸລະກິດເປັນຈັ່ງໃດ

◆ What's your name?   jâo sɯɯ nyăng. ເຈົ້າຊື່ຫຍັງ?

◆ My name is _____.   kɔ̀i sɯɯ _____..
                 ຂ້ອຍຊື່ _____.

◆ What kind of work do   jâo het wîak nyăng.
     you do?   ເຈົ້າເຮັດວຽກຫຍັງ?

◆ I'm _____.   kɔ̀i bpèn _____.
                 ຂ້ອຍເປັນ _____.

❐ A doctor   taan-mɔ̌ɔ ທ່ານໝໍ

❐ An engineer   wit-sa-wa-gɔɔn ວິສະວະກອນ

❐ A student   nak-hían ນັກຮຽນ

❐ A professor   sàat-sa-dàa-jàan ສາດສະດາຈານ

❐ A tourist   nak-tông-tiao ນັກທ່ອງທ່ຽວ

❐ A business person   nak-tu-la-gĭt ນັກທຸລະກິດ

◆ Where are you from?   jâo máa jàak săi.
                 ເຈົ້າມາຈາກໃສ?

◆ What country are   jâo máa jàak bpa-têet dăi.
     you from?   ເຈົ້າມາຈາກປະເທດໃດ?

◆ I'm from _____.   kɔ̀i máa jàak _____.
                 ຂ້ອຍມາຈາກ _____.

❐ America   àa-mée-li-gàa ອາເມລິກາ

❐ Japan   nyii-bpun ຍີ່ປຸ່ນ

❐ England   àng-gĭt ອັງກິດ

❐ Germany   yɔ́ɔi-la-mán ເຍຍລະມັນ

❐ Australia   ot-sa-dtràa-líi ອົດສະຕຣາລີ

◆ Do you like Laos?   jâo mak múang láao bɔɔ.

ເຈົ້າມັກເມືອງລາວບໍ່?

◆ Yes, very much.   mak lǎai. ມັກຫລາຍ.

◆ Do you like Lao food?   jâo mak àa-hǎan láao bɔɔ.

ເຈົ້າມັກອາຫານລາວບໍ່?

◆ Yes, I think it's very good. mak kɔ̀i kit waa sêɛp lǎai.

ມັກ, ຂ້ອຍຄິດວ່າແຊບຫລາຍ.

◆ I think it's too spicy for me. kɔ̀i kit waa mán pět gɔ̀ən
                                 bpài sǎm lǎp kɔ̀i.

ຂ້ອຍຄິດວ່າມັນເຜັດເກີນໄປສຳລັບຂ້ອຍ.

◆ What do you think about   jâo kit waa múang láao
     Laos?   bpèn jang dǎi.

ເຈົ້າຄິດວ່າເມືອງລາວເປັນຈັ່ງໃດ?

◆ I think it's very beautiful.   kɔ̀i kit waa ngáam laai.

ຂ້ອຍຄິດວ່າງາມຫລາຍ.

◆ I think it's a hard place   kɔ̀i kit waa yuu nyâak.
     to live in.

ຂ້ອຍຄິດວ່າມັນຢູ່ຍາກ.

◆ I think it's very hot.   kɔ̀i kit waa hɔ̀ɔn lǎai.

ຂ້ອຍຄິດວ່າຮ້ອນຫລາຍ.

◆ I like Vientiane.   kɔ̀i mak wíang-jàn.

ຂ້ອຍມັກວຽງຈັນ.

◆ I don't like Vientiane.   kɔ̀i bɔɔ mak wíang-jàn.

ຂ້ອຍບໍ່ມັກວຽງຈັນ.

◆ Can you speak Lao?   jâo wâo láao dâi bɔɔ.

ເຈົ້າເວົ້າລາວໄດ້ບໍ່?

◆ Can you speak Thai?   jâo wâo tái dâi bɔɔ.

ເຈົ້າເວົ້າໄທໄດ້ບໍ່?

◆ Can you speak English?   jâo wâo páa-sǎa àng-gǐt
                                 dâi bɔɔ. ເຈົ້າເວົ້າພາສາອັງກິດໄດ້ບໍ່?

◆ (Please) speak more slowly.

(ga-lu-náa) wâo sâa-sâa dɛɛ.

(ກະລຸນາ) ເວົ້າຊ້າໆແດ່.

◆ A little bit.

jăk nɔi. ຈັກໜ່ອຍ.

◆ I'm studying Lao.

kɔi gàm-làng hían páa-săa láao.

ຂ້ອຍກຳລັງຮຽນພາສາລາວ.

◆ I'm studying Lao from
   this book.

kɔi gàm-làng hían páa-săa.
láao jàak bpûm hŭa nîi

ຂ້ອຍກຳລັງຮຽນພາສາລາວຈາກປຶ້ມຫົວນີ້.

◆ Where did you learn English?

jâo hían páa-săa àng-gĭt
yuu-sai.

ເຈົ້າຮຽນພາສາອັງກິດຢູ່ໃສ?

◆ How do you say this in Lao?

kám nîi páa-săa láao waa
jang-dǎi.

ຄຳນີ້ພາສາລາວວ່າຈັ່ງໃດ?

◆ How do you read this in Lao?

kám nîi páa-săa láao waa
jang dǎi.

ຄຳນີ້ພາສາລາວອ່ານວ່າຈັ່ງໃດ?

◆ What does this mean?

àn nîi măai-kwáam waa
jang dǎi.

ອັນນີ້ໝາຍຄວາມວ່າຈັ່ງໃດ?

◆ What does ____ mean?

____ măai-kwáam waa
jang dǎi.

____ ໝາຍຄວາມວ່າຈັ່ງໃດ?

◆ How old are you?

jâo àa-nyu tao dǎi.

ເຈົ້າອາຍຸເທົ່າໃດ?

◆ I'm _____ years old.

kɔi àa-nyu _____ bpìi.

ຂ້ອຍອາຍຸ_____ ປີ.

◆ Where do you live?
   (Where is your house?)

hŭan jâo yuu săi.

ເຮືອນເຈົ້າຢູ່ໃສ?

◆ I live in _____.   kɔ̀i yuu tii _____.

ຂ້ອຍຢູ່ທີ່ _____.

◆ My house is_____.   hɯ́an kɔ̀i yuu _____.

ເຮືອນຂ້ອຍຢູ່ _____.

◆ My house is not far from here.   hɯ́an kɔ̀i yuu bɔɔ gài jàak nîi.

ເຮືອນຂ້ອຍຢູ່ບໍ່ໄກຈາກນີ້.

◆ Do you have brothers or   jâo mɯ́i pii nɔ̂ɔng bɔɔ.
   sisters?
ເຈົ້າມີພີ່ນ້ອງບໍ່?

◆ How many brothers and   jâo mɯ́i pii nɔ̂ɔng jǎk kón.
   sisters do you have?
ເຈົ້າມີພີ່ນ້ອງຈັກຄົນ?

◆ Are you married?   jâo dtɛng-ngáan lɛ̂ɛo bɔɔ.

ເຈົ້າແຕ່ງງານແລ້ວບໍ່?

◆ I'm married.   kɔ̀i dtɛng-ngáan lɛ̂ɛo.

ຂ້ອຍແຕ່ງງານແລ້ວ.

◆ I'm not married.   kɔ̀i nyáng bɔɔ tán
                                          dtɛng-ngáan tɯa.
ຂ້ອຍຍັງບໍ່ທັນແຕ່ງງານເທື່ອ.

◆ I'm divorced.   kɔ̀i bpèn (pɔɔ/mɛɛ) hâang.

ຂ້ອຍເປັນ (ພໍ່/ແມ່) ຮ້າງ.

◆ I'm single.   kɔ̀i bpèn sòot.

ຂ້ອຍເປັນໂສດ.

◆ How's your family?   kɔ̂ɔp-kúa jâo bpèn jang-dai.

ຄອບຄົວເຈົ້າເປັນຈັ່ງໃດ?

◆ How's the weather?   àa-gàat bpèn jang-dǎi.

ອາກາດເປັນຈັ່ງໃດ?

◆ It's hot.   hɔ̂ɔn. ຮ້ອນ.

◆ It's cold.   nǎao. ໜາວ.

◆ Are you free tonight?   mɯ̀ɯ lɛ́ɛng nîi jâo waang bɔɔ.

ມື້ແລງນີ້ເຈົ້າຫວ່າງບໍ່?

◆ Can I see you tomorrow?   kɔ̀i pop jâo mûu uun
                                                dâi bɔɔ.
                                                ຂ້ອຍພົບເຈົ້າມື້ອື່ນໄດ້ບໍ່?

◆ Are you free next Friday   kúun wán sǔk nàa jâo
   night?   waang bɔɔ.
                                                ຄືນວັນສຸກໜ້າເຈົ້າຫວ່າງບໍ່?

◆ Can you teach me Lao?   jâo sɔ̌ɔn páa-sǎa láao hài
                                                kɔ̀i dâi bɔɔ.
                                                ເຈົ້າສອນພາສາລາວໃຫ້ຂ້ອຍໄດ້ບໍ່?

◆ I like _____.   kɔ̀i mak _____.
                                                ຂ້ອຍມັກ _____.

◆ I don't like _____.   kɔ̀i bɔɔ mak _____.
                                                ຂ້ອຍບໍ່ມັກ _____.

◆ I like Lao people.   kɔ̀i mak kón láao.
                                                ຂ້ອຍມັກຄົນລາວ.

◆ I don't like lazy people.   kɔ̀i bɔɔ mak kón kîi-kâan.
                                                ຂ້ອຍບໍ່ມັກຄົນຂີ້ຄ້ານ.

◆ You are kind.   jâo jài-dìi. ເຈົ້າໃຈດີ.

◆ Where are you staying?   jâo pak yuu sǎi. ເຈົ້າພັກຢູ່ໃສ?

◆ I'm staying at the Grand Hotel. kɔ̀i pak yuu hóong-hέεm grὲεn.
                                                ຂ້ອຍພັກຢູ່ໂຮງແຣມແກຣນ.

◆ I enjoy talking with you.   kɔ̀i mak lóm gǎp jâo.
                                                  ຂ້ອຍມັກລົມກັບເຈົ້າ.

◆ Here is my address.   nîi mεεn tii-yuu kɔ̌ong kɔ̀i.
                                                ນີ້ແມ່ນທີ່ຢູ່ຂອງຂ້ອຍ.

◆ Here is my phone number.   nîi mεεn lêek tóo kɔ̌ong kɔ̀i.
                                                ນີ້ແມ່ນເລກໂທຂອງຂ້ອຍ.

◆ Can I have your address?   kɔ̀i kɔ̌ɔ tii-yuu jâo dâi bɔɔ.
                                                ຂ້ອຍຂໍທີ່ຢູ່ເຈົ້າໄດ້ບໍ່?

◆ Can I have your phone number? kɔ̀i kɔ̌ɔ nâam-bəə-tóo-la-
            săp jâo dâi bɔɔ.
            ຂ້ອຍຂໍເບີໂທລະສັບເຈົ້າໄດ້ບໍ່?

◆ Give me a call.   tóo hǎa kɔ̀i dɛɛ də́ə.
            ໂທຫາຂ້ອຍແດ່ເດີ.

◆ I will give you a call.   kɔ̀i ja tóo hǎa jâo.
            ຂ້ອຍຈະໂທຫາເຈົ້າ.

◆ Can I call you?   kɔ̀i tóo hǎa jâo dâi bɔɔ.
            ຂ້ອຍໂທຫາເຈົ້າໄດ້ບໍ່?

◆ I want to see you again.   kɔ̀i yàak pop jâo ìik.
            ຂ້ອຍຢາກພົບເຈົ້າອີກ.

◆ I like you.   kɔ̀i mak jâo. ຂ້ອຍມັກເຈົ້າ.

◆ I'm leaving tomorrow.   kɔ̀i ja bpài mʉ̂ʉ-ʉʉn.
            ຂ້ອຍຈະໄປມື້ອື່ນ.

◆ I'm going back to my   àa-tit nàa kɔ̀i ja gǎp kʉ́ʉn
  country next week.   bpa-têet kɔ̌ɔng kɔ̀i.
            ອາທິດໜ້າ ຂ້ອຍຈະກັບຄືນປະເທດຂອງຂ້ອຍ.

◆ I will come to Laos again.   kɔ̀i ja máa mʉang láao ìik.
            ຂ້ອຍຈະມາເມືອງລາວອີກ.

◆ I will think about you.   kɔ̀i ja kit hɔ̂ɔt jâo.
            ຂ້ອຍຈະຄິດຮອດເຈົ້າ.

◆ I will miss you.   kɔ̀i kóng ja kit hɔ̂ɔt jâo.
            ຂ້ອຍຄົງຈະ ຄິດຮອດເຈົ້າ.

◆ I will keep in touch.   kɔ̀i ja dtĭt-dtɔɔ hǎa jâo
            lʉ̂ai- lʉ̂ai.
            ຂ້ອຍຈະຕິດຕໍ່ຫາເຈົ້າເລື້ອຍໆ.

◆ Don't forget me.   yaa lʉ́ʉm kɔ̀i də́ə. ຢ່າລືມຂ້ອຍເດີ.

In a Restaurant

◆ I want to order ____.

kɔ̀i yàak sang ____.

ຂ້ອຍປາກສັ່ງ ____.

◆ What would you like to eat?

jâo yàak gìn nyǎng.

ເຈົ້າປາກກິນຫຍັງ?

◆ What would you like to drink?

jâo yàak dɯɯm nyǎng.

ເຈົ້າປາກກິ່ມຫຍັງ?

◆ I'd like a glass of water.

kɔ̀i yàak dɯɯm nâam jɔɔk
nɯng. ຂ້ອຍປາກກິ່ມນ້ຳຈອກນຶ່ງ.

◆ I'd like one serving of
    fried rice.

kɔ̀i yàak dâi kào pǎt jàan
nɯng. ຂ້ອຍປາກໄດ້ເຂົ້າຜັດຈານນຶ່ງ.

◆ I'd like some ice.

kɔ̀i yàak dâi nâam gɔɔn.

ຂ້ອຍປາກໄດ້ນ້ຳກ້ອນ.

◆ Is it spicy?

mán pět bɔɔ. ມັນເຜັດບໍ່?

◆ This is too spicy.

àn-nîi pět pôot. ອັນນີ້ເຜັດໂພດ.

◆ This is not spicy.

àn-nîi bɔɔ pět. ອັນນີ້ບໍ່ເຜັດ.

◆ Is it delicious?

àn-nîi sɛ̂ɛp bɔɔ. ອັນນີ້ແຊບບໍ່?

◆ It's delicious.

sɛ̂ɛp. ແຊບ.

◆ It's not delicious.

bɔɔ sɛ̂ɛp. ບໍ່ແຊບ.

◆ The food is very delicious.

àa-hǎan sɛ̂ɛp lǎai.

ອາຫານແຊບຫລາຍ.

◆ I like Lao food.

kɔ̀i mak àa-hǎan láao.

ຂ້ອຍມັກອາຫານລາວ.

◆ I want some dessert.

kɔ̀i yàak gìn kɔ̌ɔng wǎan.

ຂ້ອຍປາກກິນຂອງຫວານ.

◆ I'm already full.

kɔ̀i im lɛ̂ɛo. ຂ້ອຍອິ່ມແລ້ວ.

◆ That's enough.

pɔɔ lɛ̂ɛo. ພໍແລ້ວ.

◆ I'm drunk.

kɔ̀i máo lào. ຂ້ອຍເມົາເຫລົ້າ.

◆ Please give me the bill.   kit ngə́n dɛɛ. ຄິດເງິນແດ່?
◆ The food is not expensive.   àa-hǎan bɔɔ péɛng.
                                     ອາຫານບໍ່ແພງ.
◆ Do I need to leave a tip?   kɔ̀i dtɔ̂ng hài tip bɔɔ.
                                     ຂ້ອຍຕ້ອງໃຫ້ທິບບໍ?
◆ Menu   mée-núu/láai-gàan-àa-hǎan
                                     ເມນູ/ລາຍການອາຫານ

❑ bake/baked   ŏp ອົບ
❑ beer   bìa ເບຍ
❑ beef   sîin-ngúa ຊີ້ນງົວ
❑ boil/boiled   dtôm ຕົ້ມ
❑ chicken   gai ໄກ່
❑ coffee   gàa-fée ກາເຟ
❑ crab   ga-bpùu ກະປູ
❑ curry   gèɛng-ga-lii ແກງກະຫລີ່
❑ dessert   kɔ̌ɔng wǎan ຂອງຫວານ
❑ delicious   sɛ̂ɛp ແຊບ
❑ duck   bpět ເປັດ
❑ eat   gìn ກິນ
❑ egg   kai ໄຂ່
❑ fish   bpàa ປາ
❑ food   àa-hǎan ອາຫານ
❑ fry/fried   jùun ຈືນ
❑ fruit   màak-mâi ໝາກໄມ້
❑ grill/grilled   bpîng ປີ້ງ
❑ ice.   nâam-gɔ̂ɔn ນ້ຳກ້ອນ
❑ noodles   fɔ̌ə ເຝີ
❑ orange juice   nâam-màak-gîang ນ້ຳໝາກກ້ຽງ
❑ pork   sîin-mǔu ຊີ້ນໝູ

☐ porridge   kào-bpìak ເຂົ້າປຽກ
☐ rice   kào ເຂົ້າ
☐ seafood   àa-hǎan-ta-lée ອາຫານທະເລ
☐ shrimp   gûng ກຸ້ງ
☐ snack   àa-hǎan-waang ອາຫານຫວ່າງ
☐ soup   gɛɛng ແກງ
☐ squid   bpàa-mǔk ປາໝຶກ
☐ sticky rice   kào-nǐao ເຂົ້າໜຽວ
☐ tea   sáa ຊາ
☐ Lao food   àa-hǎan-láao ອາຫານລາວ
☐ turkey   gai-ngúang ໄກ່ງວງ
☐ vegetable   pǎk ຜັກ
☐ vegetarian   àa-hǎan-pǎk/jèe ອາຫານຜັກ/ເຈ
☐ whisky   lào ເຫຼົ້າ
☐ wine   lào-wɛ́ɛng ເຫຼົ້າແວງ

Expressing Needs and Feelings

◆   I'm hungry.   kɔ̀i hǐu kào/kɔ̀i yàak kào.
                            ຂ້ອຍຫິວເຂົ້າ/ຂ້ອຍປາກເຂົ້າ.

◆   I'm thirsty.   kɔ̀i yàak nâm. ຂ້ອຍປາກນ້ຳ.

◆   I'm tired.   kɔ̀i mɯai. ຂ້ອຍເມື່ອຍ.

◆   I'm exhausted.   kɔ̀i hûu-sǔk mǒt-hɛ́ɛng.
                            ຂ້ອຍຮູ້ສຶກໝົດແຮງ.

◆   I'm sleepy.   kɔ̀i ngǎo-nɔ́ɔn. ຂ້ອຍເຫງົານອນ.

◆   I'm excited.   kɔ̀i dtɯɯn-dtên. ຂ້ອຍຕື່ນເຕັ້ນ.

◆   I'm hot.   kɔ̀i hɔ̂ɔn. ຂ້ອຍຮ້ອນ.

◆   I'm cold.   kɔ̀i nǎao. ຂ້ອຍໜາວ.

◆   I feel sick.   kɔ̀i bɔɔ sa-bàai. ຂ້ອຍບໍ່ສະບາຍ.

◆   I have a headache.   kɔ̀i jĕp hǔa. ຂ້ອຍເຈັບຫົວ.

◆   I have a stomachache.   kɔ̀i jĕp tɔ̂ɔng. ຂ້ອຍເຈັບທ້ອງ.

◆   I have diarrhea.   kɔ̀i mǐi àa-gàan-sǔ-tɔ̂ɔng.
                            ຂ້ອຍມີອາການສຸທ້ອງ.

◆   I have jet-lag.   kɔ̀i bpǎp wée-láa bɔɔ tán.
                            ຂ້ອຍປັບເວລາບໍ່ທັນ.

◆   I need some medicine.   kɔ̀i yàak dâi yàa. ຂ້ອຍປາກໄດ້ຢາ.

◆   I need some rest.   kɔ̀i yàak pak jǎk nɔi.
                            ຂ້ອຍປາກພັກຈັກໜ່ອຍ.

◆   I want to see a doctor. kɔ̀i yàak bpài hǎa taan mɔ̌ɔ.
                            ຂ້ອຍປາກໄປຫາທ່ານໝໍ.

◆   I need help.   kɔ̀i dtɔ̂ng gàan kwáam sɔɔi-lǔa.
                            ຂ້ອຍຕ້ອງການການຊ່ອຍເຫລືອ.

◆   Come here.   máa-nîi. ມານີ້.

◆   Help!   sɔɔi dɛɛ. ຊ່ອຍແດ່!

◆   Watch out!   la-wáng. ລະວັງ!

◆ I want to drink some water.   kɔ̀i yàak dʉ̀ʉm nâm.
ຂ້ອຍຢາກກິ່ມນ້ຳ.

◆ I want to have some   kɔ̀i yàak gìn bìa.
   beer.   ຂ້ອຍຢາກກິນເບຍ.

◆ I want to have a cup   kɔ̀i yàak gìn gàa-fée jɔ̀ɔk nʉ̀ng.
   of coffee.   ຂ້ອຍຢາກກິນກາເຟຈອກໜຶ່ງ.

◆ I want to buy some   kɔ̀i yàak sʉ́ʉ yàa-sùup.
   cigarettes.   ຂ້ອຍຢາກຊື້ຢາສູບ.

◆ I want to buy some   kɔ̀i yàak sʉ́ʉ yàa.
   medicine.   ຂ້ອຍຢາກຊື້ຢາ.

◆ I want to use the restroom.   kɔ̀i yàak kào hɔ̀ng nâam.
ຂ້ອຍຢາກເຂົ້າຫ້ອງນ້ຳ.

◆ Where is the restroom?   hɔ̀ng-nâam yuu sǎi. ຫ້ອງນ້ຳຢູ່ໃສ?

◆ It's too loud.   sǐang dàng pôot. ສຽງດັງໂພດ.

◆ Can you turn down   jâo pɔn ɛ̀ɛ lóng dɛɛ
   the air-conditioner?   dâi bɔɔ. ເຈົ້າຜ່ອນແອລົງແດກໄດ້ບໍ່?

◆ Can you turn up   jâo bpə̀ət ɛ̀ɛ kʉ̀n dtʉ̀ʉm dɛɛ
   the air-conditioner?   dâi bɔɔ. ເຈົ້າເປີກແອຂຶ້ນຕື່ມແດກໄດ້ບໍ່?

◆ Turn on the fan.   bpə̀ət pat-lóm. ເປີດພັດລົມ.

◆ It's very hot and stuffy   yuu nîi hɔ̀ɔn lɛ ǒp-âo
   in here.   lǎai. ຢູ່ນີ້ຮ້ອນແລະອົບເອົ້າຫລາຍ.

◆ Can I use the telephone?   kɔ̀i kɔ̌ɔ sǎi tóo-la-sǎp dɛɛ
   dâi bɔɔ. ຂ້ອຍຂໍໃຊ້ໂທລະສັບແດກໄດ້ບໍ່?

◆ Can I have more water?   kɔ̀i kɔ̌ɔ nâm dtʉ̀ʉm
   ìik dɛɛ. ຂ້ອຍຂໍນ້ຳຕື່ມອີກແດກ.

◆ I'm lost.   kɔ̀i lǒng táang. ຂ້ອຍຫລົງທາງ.

◆ How do I go to ____?   kɔ̀i ja bpài ____ dâi jang
   dǎi. ຂ້ອຍຈະໄປ ____ ໄດ້ຈັ່ງໃດ?

◆ I need more money.

kɔ̀i dtɔ̂ng gàan ngə́n dtɨɨm ìik.

ຂ້ອຍຕ້ອງການເງິນຕື່ມອີກ.

◆ I need to go to the bank.

kɔ̀i dtɔ̂ng bpài ta-náa-káan.

ຂ້ອຍຕ້ອງໄປທະນາຄານ.

◆ I need to exchange money.

kɔ̀i yàak bpian ngə́n.

ຂ້ອຍຢາກປ່ຽນເງິນ.

◆ I need to call a taxi.

kɔ̀i dtɔ̂ng tóo ɔ̂ɔn lot dtak-sîi.

ຂ້ອຍຕ້ອງໂທເອີ້ນລົດຕັກຊີ.

◆ I want to go home.

kɔ̀i yàak bpài hŭan.

ຂ້ອຍຢາກໄປເຮືອນ.

◆ I want to _____ (verb).

kɔ̀i dtɔ̂ng gàan_____.

ຂ້ອຍຕ້ອງການ _____.

kɔ̀i yàak ___.   ຂ້ອຍຢາກ ____.

◆ I want _____ (noun).

kɔ̀i dtɔ̂ng-gàan _____. /

kɔ̀i yàak dâi _____.

ຂ້ອຍຕ້ອງການ _____. /

ຂ້ອຍຢາກໄດ້ _____.

◆ Give me _____.

ào _____ hài kɔ̀i dɛɛ.

ເອົາ _____ ໃຫ້ຂ້ອຍແດ່.

◆ Give me a pen.

kɔ̌ɔ bpàak-gàa dɛɛ. ຂໍປາກກາແດ່.

◆ I have a question.

kɔ̀i mǐi kám-tǎam. ຂ້ອຍມີຄຳຖາມ.

◆ I have to leave.

kɔ̀i dtɔ̂ng bpài lɛ̂ɛo là.

ຂ້ອຍຕ້ອງໄປແລ້ວລະ.

◆ I have to go back to
   my hotel.

kɔ̀i dtɔ̂ng gǎp hóong-hɛ́ɛm
   lɛ̂ɛo là. ຂ້ອຍຕ້ອງກັບໂຮງແຮມແລ້ວລະ.

◆ I'm leaving tomorrow.

kɔ̀i ja mɨ̌a mɨ̌ɨ-ɨɨn.

ຂ້ອຍຈະເມືອມື້ອື່ນ.

◆ I'm going back to
   my country.

kɔ̀i ja gǎp kɨɨn bpa-têet
   kɔ̌ɔng kɔ̀i.

ຂ້ອຍຈະກັບຄືນປະເທດຂອງຂ້ອຍ.

◆ I understand.
kɔ̀i kào jài. ຂ້ອຍເຂົ້າໃຈ.

◆ I don't understand.
kɔ̀i bɔɔ kào jài. ຂ້ອຍບໍ່ເຂົ້າໃຈ.

◆ I don't know.
kɔ̀i bɔɔ hûu. ຂ້ອຍບໍ່ຮູ້.

◆ I think so, too.
kɔ̀i kit jang-sân kúu-gàn.
ຂ້ອຍຄິດຈັ່ງຊັ້ນຄືກັນ.

◆ I don't think so.
kɔ̀i bɔɔ kit nɛ́ɛo nân.
ຂ້ອຍບໍ່ຄິດແນວນັ້ນ.

◆ I believe you.
kɔ̀i sʉa jâo. ຂ້ອຍເຊື່ອເຈົ້າ.

◆ I don't believe you.
kɔ̀i bɔɔ sʉa jâo. ຂ້ອຍບໍ່ເຊື່ອເຈົ້າ.

◆ I'm sure.
kɔ̀i nɛɛ-jài. ຂ້ອຍແນ່ໃຈ.

◆ I'm not sure.
kɔ̀i bɔɔ nɛɛ-jài. ຂ້ອຍບໍ່ແນ່ໃຈ.

◆ I'm joking.
kɔ̀i wâo lìn. ຂ້ອຍເວົ້າຫຼິ້ນ.

◆ I like it.
kɔ̀i mak. ຂ້ອຍມັກ.

◆ I like it very much.
kɔ̀i mak lǎai. ຂ້ອຍມັກຫຼາຍ.

◆ I don't like it.
kɔ̀i bɔɔ mak. ຂ້ອຍບໍ່ມັກ.

◆ I forgot.
kɔ̀i lúum. ຂ້ອຍລືມ.

◆ I remember.
kɔ̀i jʉʉ dâi. ຂ້ອຍຈື່ໄດ້.

◆ I don't remember.
kɔ̀i jʉʉ bɔɔ dâi. ຂ້ອຍຈື່ບໍ່ໄດ້.

◆ Is that right?
tʉʉk bɔɔ. ຖືກບໍ່?

◆ No problem.
bɔɔ míi bàn-hǎa. ບໍ່ມີບັນຫາ.

◆ That's interesting.
nàa-sǒn-jài. ໜ້າສົນໃຈ.

◆ Let's go.
bpài gàn tɔ. ໄປກັນເຖາະ.

◆ Are you ready/finished?
jâo lɛ̂ɛo lɛ̂ɛo bɔɔ.
ເຈົ້າແລ້ວແລ້ວບໍ່?

◆ May I smoke?
kɔ̀i kɔ̌ɔ sùup yàa dâi bɔɔ.
ຂ້ອຍຂໍສູບຢາໄດ້ບໍ່?

◆ No smoking.
hàam sùup yàa. ຫ້າມສູບຢາ.

◆ I'm ready.
kɔ̀i pɔ̂ɔm lɛ̂ɛo. ຂ້ອຍພ້ອມແລ້ວ.

◆ I'm not ready.   kɔ̀i nyáng bɔɔ pɔ̂ɔm.
                                     ຂ້ອຍຍັງບໍ່ພ້ອມ.

◆ I'm busy.   kɔ̀i káa wîak. ຂ້ອຍຄາວຽກ.
◆ I'm happy.   kɔ̀i mîi kwáam sŭk.
                                     ຂ້ອຍມີຄວາມສຸກ.

◆ I'm enjoying myself.   kɔ̀i muan. ຂ້ອຍມ່ວນ.
◆ I'm sad.   kɔ̀i sào-jài. ຂ້ອຍເສົ້າໃຈ.
◆ I'm fine.   kɔ̀i sa-bàai-dìi. ຂ້ອຍສະບາຍດີ.
◆ I'm angry.   kɔ̀i jài hâai. ຂ້ອຍໃຈຮ້າຍ.
◆ I'm mad at you.   kɔ̀i kîat hài jâo. ຂ້ອຍຄຽດໃສ່ເຈົ້າ.
◆ I'm lonely.   kɔ̀i ngǎo. ຂ້ອຍເຫງົາ.
◆ I'm surprised.   kɔ̀i bpa-làat-jài. ຂ້ອຍປະຫລາດໃຈ.
◆ I'm disappointed.   kɔ̀i pĭt-wǎng. ຂ້ອຍຜິດຫວັງ.
◆ I'm worried.   kɔ̀i gàng-wón-jài. ຂ້ອຍກັງວົນໃຈ.
◆ I'm worried about you.   kɔ̀i bpèn-huang jâo.
                                     ຂ້ອຍເປັນຫ່ວງເຈົ້າ.

◆ I'm confused.   kɔ̀i sǎp-sŏn. ຂ້ອຍສັບສົນ.
◆ I'm hurt (emotionally).   kɔ̀i jĕp-jài. ຂ້ອຍເຈັບໃຈ.
◆ It's embarrassing.   mán bpèn-dtɛɛ-nàa-àai.
                                     ມັນເປັນແຕ່ໜ້າອາຍ.

◆ I'm desperate.   kɔ̀i mŏt-wǎng. ຂ້ອຍໝົດຫວັງ.
◆ I envy you.   kɔ̀i ĭt-sǎa-jâo. ຂ້ອຍອິດສາເຈົ້າ.
◆ I have a broken heart.   kɔ̀i ŏk-hǎk. ຂ້ອຍອົກຫັກ.
◆ I don't want to promise.   kɔ̀i bɔɔ yàak hài sǎn-nyáa.
                                     ຂ້ອຍບໍ່ຢາກໃຫ້ສັນຍາ.

◆ It's boring.   bpèn-dtàa-bɯa. ເປັນຕາເບື່ອ.
◆ I am homesick.   kɔ̀i kit-hɔ̂ɔt bâan.
                                     ຂ້ອຍຄຶດຮອດບ້ານ.

◆ I made a mistake.   kɔ̀i het pĭt-pâat bpài.
                                     ຂ້ອຍເຮັດຜິດພາດໄປ.

◆ I agree with you.   kɔ̀i hěn pɔ̂ɔm nám jâo.

ຂ້ອຍເຫັນພ້ອມນຳເຈົ້າ.

◆ I don't agree with you.   kɔ̀i bɔɔ hěn pɔ̂ɔm nám jâo.

ຂ້ອຍບໍ່ເຫັນພ້ອມນຳເຈົ້າ.

◆ Listen!   fáng/fáng nîi gɔɔn. ຟັງ! /ຟັງນີ້ກ່ອນ!

◆ Look!   bəng hàn/bəng mɛ̌ɛ/bəng dtǐi.

ເບິ່ງຫັນ! /ເບິ່ງແມ່! /ເບິ່ງຕີ!

◆ A little bit.   nɔ̀i nɯng. ໜ້ອຍນຶ່ງ.

◆ Very. A lot.   lǎai. ຫລາຍ.

◆ Speak more slowly.   wâo sâa-sâa gwaa nîi.

ເວົ້າຊ້າໆກວ່ານີ້.

◆ Speak up!   wâo dàng-dàng. ເວົ້າດັງໆ!

◆ Say it again.   wâo ìik tɯa/kɯ̌ɯn wâo ìik duu.

ເວົ້າອີກເທື່ອ/ຄືນເວົ້າອີກດູ.

◆ I can't hear.   kɔ̀i bɔɔ dâi nyín. ຂ້ອຍບໍ່ໄດ້ຍິນ.

◆ Be careful.   la-wáng. ລະວັງ.

◆ Wait a minute.   tàa bǔt-nɯng. ຖ້າບຶດນຶ່ງ.

◆ It's too loud.   sǐang-dàng pôot. ສຽງດັງໂພດ.

◆ Happy Birthday!   sǔk-sǎn wán gəət.

ສຸກສັນວັນເກີດ!

◆ Merry Christmas!   sǔk-sǎn wán kit-sa-mâat.

ສຸກສັນວັນຄຣິສມາສ!

◆ Congratulations!   kɔ̌ɔ sa-dɛ̀ɛng kwáam nyín

dǐi nám.

ຂໍສະແດງຄວາມຍິນດີນຳ!

◆ I'm sorry to hear that.   kɔ̀i sǐa-jài dûai. ຂ້ອຍເສຍໃຈດ້ວຍ.

◆ I wish you happiness.   kɔ̌ɔ hâi mǐi kwáam sǔk.

ຂໍໃຫ້ມີຄວາມສຸກ.

◆   I wish you lots of happiness.   kɔ̌ɔ hài mîi kwáam-sǔk
                                         lǎai-lǎai.

ຂໍໃຫ້ມີຄວາມສຸກຫລາຍໆ.

◆   I'm happy for you.   kɔ̀i dìi-jài nám.

ຂ້ອຍດີໃຈນຳ.

◆   I'm sorry for you.   kɔ̀i sǐa-jài nám.

ຂ້ອຍເສຍໃຈນຳ.

◆   Amen.   àa-méen/sǎa-tu.

ອາເມນ/ສາທຸ

◆   Wow!   ôo.

ໂອ້ !

◆   Good luck.   sôok-dìi/kɔ̌ɔ hài sôok-dìi.

ໂຊກດີ/ຂໍໃຫ້ໂຊກດີ .

Appendix II
Summary of the Lao Writing System

Lao Spelling Inconsistencies

You may encounter different ways of spelling a word in different dictionaries or by different people and wonder about the inconsistencies. Many Lao people left the country because of the political situation in the 1970's. They are used to the old writing system, which is more complicated (it is similar to written Thai) than the current system. Other Lao people may write words exactly the way they hear them, regardless of the official spelling. The Lao Ministry of Education has standardized the spelling and writing system but you will still see many variants.

Here are some examples of spelling variations that you may come across:

ເບຍ (beer) may be seen written as ເບຍ, ເບຽ, ເບ້ຍ, ເບ້ຽ.
ເລື່ອງ (story, matter) may be seen written as ເລື້ອງ, ເລື່ອງ.
ໄລຍະ (distance) may be seen written as ໄລຍະ, ລະຍະ.
ເພີ່ມ (add) may be seen written as ເພີ້ມ, ເພິ່ມ.
ດຶ່ມ (ground) may be seen written as ດຶມ, ດຶ່ມ.
ໂລກ (world, disease) may be seen written as ໂລກ, ໂຣກ.
ຫລາຍ (many) may be seen written as ຫລາຍ, ຫຼາຍ.
ຮັບ (receive) may be seen written as ຮັບ, ຣັບ, ລັບ.
ໂຮງແຮມ (hotel) may be seen written as ໂຮງແຮມ, ໂຮງແຣມ.
ກຳນົດ (set, establish) may be seen written as ກຳນົດ, ກຳໜົດ.

The letter ຣ /r/ is not officially listed in the current Lao writing system. However, you will see it written sporadically. Lao people no longer pronounce the /r/, having replaced it entirely with the /l/ sound. Therefore, it was removed from the alphabet during the Ministry of Education's standardization of the writing system and replaced with ລ /l/ wherever it had occurred. Sometimes people still use the ຣ to transliterate foreign words into Lao. For example, ຝຣັ່ງ (foreigner or Caucasian) is often written with the ຣ, but is still pronounced with the /l/ sound.

26 Lao Consonants in Alphabetical Order

ໜ°   ຂ•   ຄ△   ງ△

ຈ°   ສ•   ຊ△   ຍ△

ດ°   ຕ°   ຖ•   ທ△

ນ△   ບ°   ປ°   ຜ•

ຝ•   ພ△   ຟ△   ມ△

ຢ°   ລ△   ວ△   ຫ•

ອ°   ຣ△

ຣ /r/ is not listed here. It is no longer officially in the Lao writing system, but may still be seen written here and there (many times with foreign words). When it occurs it is pronounced as /l/.

• 6 High consonants

◇ 8 Mid consonants

△ 12 Low consonants

Consonant	Consonant Name	Sound
ກ°	ກ ໄກ່ gɔ̌ɔ gai - chicken	/g/
ຂ•	ຂ ໄຂ່ kɔ̌ɔ kai - egg	/k/
ຄᐞ	ຄ ຄວາຍ kɔ̌ɔ kwáai - buffalo	/k/
ງᐞ	ງ ງົວ ngɔ̌ɔ ngúa - cow	/ng/
ຈ°	ຈ ຈອກ jɔ̌ɔ jɔ̀ɔk - cup, glass	/j/
ສ•	ສ ເສືອ sɔ̌ɔ sǔa - tiger	/s/
ຊᐞ	ຊ ຊ້າງ sɔ̌ɔ sâang - elephant	/s/
ຍᐞ	ຍ ຍຸງ nyɔ̌ɔ nyúng - mosquito	/ny/
ດ°	ດ ເດັກ dɔ̌ɔ děk - child	/d/
ຕ°	ຕ ຕາ dtɔ̌ɔ dtàa - eye	/dt/
ຖ•	ຖ ຖົງ tɔ̌ɔ tǒng - bag	/t/
ທᐞ	ທ ທຸງ tɔ̌ɔ túng - flag	/t/
ນᐞ	ນ ນົກ nɔ̌ɔ nok - bird	/n/
ບ°	ບ ແບ້ bɔ̌ɔ bêɛ - goat	/b/

ປ˚   ປ ປາ   bpɔ̌ɔ bpàa - fish   /bp/

ຜ˙   ຜ ເຜິ້ງ   pɔ̌ɔ pɔ̀ng - bee   /p/

ຟ˙   ຟ ຝົນ   fɔ̌ɔ fǒn - rain   /f/

ພᐃ   ພ ພູ   pɔ̌ɔ púu - mountain   /p/

ຟᐃ   ຟ ໄຟ   fɔ̌ɔ faí - fire   /f/

ມᐃ   ມ ແມວ   mɔ̌ɔ mέɛo - cat   /m/

ຢ˚   ຢ ຢາ   yɔ̌ɔ yàa - medicine   /y/

ລᐃ   ລ ລິງ   lɔ̌ɔ líng - monkey   /l/

ວᐃ   ວ ວີ   wɔ̌ɔ wíi - fan   /w/

ຫ˙   ຫ ຫ່ານ   hɔ̌ɔ haan - goose   /h/

ອ˚   ອ ໂອ   ɔ̌ɔ òo - bowl   /ɔ/

ຮᐃ   ຮ ເຮືອນ   hɔ̌ɔ húan - house   /h/

˙ 6 High consonants
˚ 8 Mid consonants
ᐃ 12 Low consonants

28 Lao Vowels in Alphabetical Order

ອະ	ອາ	ອິ	ອີ
ອຶ	ອື	ອຸ	ອູ
ເອະ	ເອ	ແອະ	ແອ
ໂອະ	ໂອ	ເອາະ	ອໍ
ເອິ	ເອີ	ເອັຍ	ເອຍ
ເອຶອ	ເອືອ	ອົວະ	ອົວ
ໄອ	ໃອ	ເອົາ	ອຳ

Lao Vowels Paired With Short and Long Counterparts

Short vowels are displayed in the left column and their counterparts (long vowels) are on the right.

Short Vowel		Long Vowel	
ອະ	/ǎ/	ອາ	/àa/
ອິ	/ǐ/	ອີ	/ìi/
ອຶ	/ʉ̌/	ອື	/ʉ̀ʉ/
ອຸ	/ǔ/	ອູ	/ùu/

ເເະ	/ĕ/	ເເ	/ēe/
ແເະ	/ɛ̆/	ແເ	/ɛ̄ɛ/
ໂເະ	/ŏ/	ໂເ	/ōo/
ເເາະ	/ɔ̆/	°	/ɔ̄ɔ/
ເ°	/ə̆/	ເ°	/ə̄ə/
ເ°ຍ	/ĭa/	ເຍ	/īa/
ເ°ຂ	/ŭa/	ເ°ຂ	/ūa/
°ɔະ	/ŭa/	°ɔ	/ūa/

The following vowels may sound either short or long, but they are categorized as long vowels for tone rule purposes. Sometimes they are called "special vowels".

ໄ°   /ài mâi-ma-laai/

ໃ°   /ài mâi-mûan/

ເ°າ   /ào/

°ຳ   /àm/

Lao Numbers

໐	ສູນ	sǔun	0
໑	ໜຶ່ງ	nɯng	1
໒	ສອງ	sɔ̌ɔng	2
໓	ສາມ	sǎam	3
໔	ສີ່	sii	4
໕	ຫ້າ	hàa	5
໖	ຫົກ	hǒk	6
໗	ເຈັດ	jĕt	7
໘	ແປດ	bpɛ̀ɛt	8
໙	ເກົ້າ	gâo	9

Appendix III
Test and Writing Exercise Answers

Test Answers

Test1

Matching (Page 26)

1. e   2. j   3. b   4. c   5. g
6. l   7. k   8. h   9. a   10. i

Translation (Page 26)

1. How are you?
2. (Do you) understand?
3. Is this a newspaper?
4. What's your name?
5. Is this a map or a pencil?

Test 2

Matching (Page 50)

1. m   2. k   3. n   4. l   5. o
6. e   7. p   8. g   9. b   10. a
11. j   12. q   13. d   14. f   15. h

Translation (Page 51)

1. The telephone is on the chair.
2. He is Chinese, not Japanese.
3. How much is this?
4. Where is the bathroom?
5. English is very difficult.

Test 3

Matching (Page 71)

1. j   2. n   3. f   4. a   5. q
6. m   7. b   8. l   9. d   10. p
11. c   12. e   13. h   14. i   15. k

Translation (Page 72)

1. Where do you work?
2. I like blue cars.
3. Do you like Lao food or Chinese food?
4. Where is he going?
5. You can write Lao very well.

Test 4

Telling Time (Page 98)

1. 6:15 a.m. or 6:15 p.m.
2. 3:00 p.m.
3. 4:30 p.m.
4. 2:35 a.m. or 2:35 p.m.
5. Exactly 3:00 p.m.
6. 4:50 a.m. or 4:50 p.m.
7. 12:20 p.m. (noon time)
8. 1:05 p.m.
9. 8:20 a.m. or 8:20 p.m.
10. 4:00 a.m.
11. 10:00 a.m.
12. Exactly noon.
13. 8:00 p.m.
14. 8:10 a.m. or 8:10 p.m.
15. 5:00 a.m.

Translation (Page 99)

1. I will go to the temple at noon.
2. He has been reading since eleven p.m.
3. We study Lao for three hours.
4. It's now one thirty p.m.
5. I eat breakfast at eight o'clock.

Test 5
Matching

Days (Page 119)
1. c   2. e   3. f   4. h   5. a   6. d   7. b   8. g

Months (Page 120)
1. i   2. e   3. l   4. a   5. g   6. h
7. j   8. c   9. f   10. k   11. d   12. b

Test 6
Matching (Page 137)

1. o   2. a   3. h   4. i   5. l
6. p   7. n   8. b   9. e   10. k
11. q   12. d   13. c   14. m   15. g

Translation (Page 138)

1. Now I'm going to the airport.
2. Normally, Mr. Kampan goes to work by train.
3. We want to have a Lao restaurant in America.
4. He has been in Thailand since June.
5. I don't like to listen to music.

Test 7

Matching (Page 156)

1. m   2. h   3. d   4. p   5. j
6. n   7. a   8. o   9. k   10. f
11. c   12. q   13. e   14. b   15. i

Translation (Page 157)

1. Whose notebook is on the table?
2. I can't swim.

3. I didn't swim.
4. He really misses Lao.
5. I think that western food is not very delicious.

Test 8

Matching (Page 174)

1. d   2. m   3. i   4. h   5. e
6. p   7. c   8. a   9. g   10. n
11. k   12. b   13. l   14. j   15. f

Translation (Page 175)

1. How many times a day do you brush your teeth?
    Twice a day.
2. He has a bad headache. He can't come to work.
3. I wash my hair everyday.
4. Somchai has dimples.
5. You have no brain.

Test 9

Matching (Page 192)
A.
1. c   2. e   3. d   4. k   5. m
6. l   7. h   8. f   9. b   10. j
B.
1. h   2. j   *3. c   4. l   5. g
6. e   7. d   8. f   9. b   10. a
C.
1. k   2. f   3. l   4. b   5. j
6. e   7. i   8. h   9. m   10. g

Translation (Page 193)

1. What kind of work does your younger brother do?
2. He is married to a Japanese.
3. Why don't you like Lao food? Because it's very hot.
4. If I don't have money, I cannot return to Laos.
5. I think that he already has a family.

Test 10

Matching (Page 219)

A.

1. c   2. l   3. i   4. e   5. k
6. a   7. b   8. f   9. h   10. g

B.

1. k   2. h   3. e   4. d   5. c
6. m   7. a   8. j   9. f   10. g

C.

1. g   2. d   3. j   4. h   5. a
6. l   7. e   8. b   9. k   10. f

Translation (Page 221)

1. Which mango is the most delicious?
   I think that this one is the most delicious.
2. How many floors are there at your house?
   There are three.
3. When will the first ship come?
   It will come tomorrow.
4. Yesterday I bought a new watch.
5. There are five elephants at the zoo.

Writing Exercise Answer

Writing Exercise 1 (Page 38)

1. ກາ   2. ໄກ່   3. ໄນ້, ໃນ້   4. ຕຸ່

5. ເອົາ   6. ໄປ່   7. ເກົ່າ   8. ຈຶ່

9. ໄຮ້, ໃຮ້   10. ດັນ   11. ໄຈ, ໃຈ   12. ເຕົ່າ

13. ໂຂ   14. ໄປ   15. ກຸ້   16. ໄປ່

17. ຈ່າ   18. ເດົາ   19. ກໍ່   20. ອ້າ

Writing Exercise 2 (Page 60)

1. ບາ   2. ແກະ   3. ເບືອ   4. ຕຸ

5. ບໍ   6. ເຈ   7. ກຶ   8. ເຈອະ

9. ອໍ   10. ຈິວ   11. ເກືອ   12. ຕໍ

13. ອຶ   14. ປະ   15. ກຶ   16. ເຕາະ

17. ເອຶ   18. ໂກະ   19. ດົວ   20. ເກຍ, ເກັຍ, ເກັຽ

Writing Exercise 3 (Page 84)

1. ຈັບ   2. ເປີດ   3. ບັງ   4. ກວມ

5. ຈຶດ   6. ເຕັມ   7. ຜຶມ   8. ກັງ

9. ເກັບ   10. ຕຶກ   11. ຄຶມ   12. ເອັມ

13. ແຄັມ   14. ຈິງ   15. ບວມ   16. ອິງ

17. ເດິມ   18. ເຈັບ   19. ປວດ   20. ບວກ

21. ກັມ   22. ຈ້ມ   23. ບັງ   24. ຊູດ

25. ກຸ້ງ   26. ຈາມ   27. ເກົ່າ   28. ຕຶມ

29. ດ້າມ   30. ໂອກ   31. ຕົ້ມ   32. ບຶບ

33. ກັ້ງ   34. ນັກ   35. ບ່າຍ   36. ໂອ່ງ
37. ຈ່າ   38. ເຈັບ   38. ແກນບ   40. ຈ່າວ

Writing Exercise 4 (Page 106)

1. ສາ   2. ຜະ   3. ສາກ   4. ຊຸກ
5. ສຽວ   6. ຕີ   7. ແຫກ   8. ຫຸບ
9. ຕຸງ   10. ຜີ່ງ   11. ຝັນ   12. ຫາບ
13. ຝາກ   14. ຝຸງ

Writing Exercise 5 (Page 122)

1. ສ່ອຍ   2. ຜິ້ງ   3. ທ້ວນ   4. ວິນ
5. ຜິ່ນ   6. ຕ່ອຍ   7. ສ່ງ   8. ຊຸກ
9. ເຜຍ   10. ຕາມ   11. ສວຍ   12. ຝັ່ງ
13. ຕິ້   14. ຝານ   15. ອາຍ   16. ເຂົ້າ
17. ທ້ອງ   18. ຝ້າຍ   19. ສາບ   20. ເສັນ

Writing Exercise 6 (Page 144)

1. ພາ   2. ໂຊ   3. ຣຳ   4. ມູ
5. ເຂຍ   6. ເລຍ   7. ເຊັຍ   8. ທົວ
9. ເຣື   10. ເຝາ   11. ຫີ   12. ບົ
13. ຝູ້   14. ເຫ   15. ລຳ   16. ລິ
17. ງາ   18. ແຜ   19. ບຳ   20. ເລັຍ

Writing Exercise 7 (Page 163)

1. ມ່ວງ   2. ນກ   3. ຄຳ   4. ຍຸງ

5. ຟີມ   6. ມີ້ວ   7. ມິກ   8. ຂອງ

9. ຟັງ   10. ແວວ   11. ຂາມ   12. ຮຽບ

13. ພູມ   14. ຮ້າມ   15. ຮາບ   16. ວ່າງ

17. ເຍື້ອງ 18. ແຂງ   19. ຄິກ   20. ເພື່ອ

Writing Exercise 8 (Page 178)

1. ທມິ່   2. ໄທນ, ໃທນ

3. ໃທຍ່, ໄທຍ່   4. ທມິ້

5. ທມັນ   6. ທລາ

7. ທຈູ່   8. ໂທລ່ງ

9. ທວັນ   10. ທວາ

About the Authors

BUASAWAN SIMMALA (ບົວສະຫວັນ ສິມມາລາ)

Buasawan Simmala was born and grew up in Vientiane, the capital of Laos. In March, 2000 she received a Fulbright Scholarship to study in the United States and subsequently received her Master's Degree in International Commerce and Policy from George Mason University in Virginia. She is currently working on her Ph.D. in urban education from the University of Wisconsin-Milwaukee. Buasawan also works part-time as a Lao language editor, interpreter and translator. She has a lot of private students and has taught Lao to foreigners from many parts of the world at the Southeast Asian Studies Summer Institute. Buasawan is proficient in Lao, Thai and Vietnamese.

BENJAWAN POOMSAN BECKER (ເບັນຈະວັນ ພູມແສນ ເບັກເກີຣ໌)

Benjawan Poomsan Becker was born in Bangkok and spent her childhood in Yasothon, a province in Northeast Thailand. Her family is ethnic Laotian, so she grew up speaking both Thai and Lao. She graduated from Khon Kaen University in Thailand in 1990, with a B.A. in English. Benjawan gained extensive experience teaching while studying for her M.A. in Japan with Berlitz Language Schools, and in the US with Thai temples, Stanford University and private students. Now she is residing in the San Francisco Bay Area where she continues to write and books on the Thai and Lao languages. Benjawan is a professional interpreter and translator in both languages. Her former Lao book includes "Lao-English English-Lao Dictionary for Non-Lao Speakers".

Language Books by Paiboon Publishing

Title: **Thai for Beginners**
Author: Benjawan Poomsan Becker ©1995
Description: Designed for either self-study or classroom use. Teaches all four
              language skills— speaking, listening (when used in conjunction
              with the audio), reading and writing . Offers clear, easy,
              step-by-step instruction building on what has been previously
              learned. Used by many Thai temples and insitutes in America.
              Cassette tapes available. Paperback. 262 pages. 6" x 8.5"

Book   US$12.95   Stock # 1001
Three Tape Set US$20.00   Stock # 1001T
Two CDs   US$20.00   Stock #1001CD

****

Title: **Thai for Intermediate Learners**
Author: Benjawan Poomsan Becker ©1998
Description: The continuation of *Thai for Beginners* . Users are expected to be
              able to read basic Thai language. There is transliteration when
              new words are introduced. Teaches reading, writing and speaking
              at a higher level. Keeps students interested with cultural facts about
              Thailand. Helps expand your Thai vocabulary in a systematic way.
              Two casettes available. Paperback. 220 pages. 6" x 8.5"

Book   US$12.95   Stock # 1002
Two Tape Set US$15.00   Stock # 1002T

****

Title: **Thai for Advanced Readers**
Author: Benjawan Poomsan Becker ©2000
Description: A book that helps students practice reading Thai at an advanced level.
              It contains reading exercises, short essays, newspaper articles, cutural
              and historical facts about Thailand and miscellaneous information
about   the Thai language. Students need to be able to read basic Thai. Two
              casette tapes available. Paperback. 210 pages. 6" x 8.5"

Book   US$12.95   Stock # 1003
Two Tape Set US$15.00   Stock # 1003T

****

Title: **Thai for Lovers**
Author: Nit & Jack Ajee ©1999
Description: An ideal book for lovers. A short cut to romantic communication
              in Thailand. There are useful sentences with their Thai translations
              throughout the book. You won't find any Thai language book more
              fun and user-friendly. **Rated R!**
              Two casettes available. Paperback. 190 pages. 6" x 8.5"

Book   US$13.95   Stock #: 1004
Two Tape Set US$17.00   Stock #: 1004T

Title:	**Thai for Gay Tourists**
Author:	Saksit Pakdeesiam ©2001
Description:	The ultimate language guide for gay and bisexual men visiting Thailand. Lots of gay oriented language, culture, commentaries and other information. Instant sentences for convenient use by gay visitors. Fun and sexy. The best way to communicate with your Thai gay friends and partners! **Rated R!** Cassette tapes available. Paperback. 220 pages. 6" x 8.5"
Book	US$13.95 Stock # 1007
Two Tape Set	US$17.00 Stock # 1007T

****

Title:	**Tai Go No Kiso**
Author:	Benjawan Poomsan Becker ©2002
Description:	Thai for Japanese Speakers. Japanese version of Thai for Beginners. Cassette tapes available. Paperback. 262 pages. 6" x 8.5"
Book	US$12.95 Stock # 1009
Three Tape Set	US$20.00 Stock # 1009T

****

Title:	**Lao-English, English-Lao Dictionary for Non-Lao Speakers**
Author:	Benjawan Poomsan Becker, Khamphan Mingbuapha ©2003
Description:	Designed to help English speakers communicate in Lao. This practical dictionary is useful both in Laos and in Northeast Thailand. Students can use it without having to learn the Lao alphabet. However, there is a comprehensive introduction to the Lao writing system and pronunciation. The transliteration system is the same as that used in Paiboon Publishing's other books. It contains most of the vocabulary used in everyday life, including basic, cultural, political and scientific terms. Paperback. 780 pages. 4.1" x 5.6"
Book	US$15.00 Stock # 1010

****

Title:	**Lao for Beginners**
Author:	Buasawan Simmala and Benjawan Poomsan Becker ©2003
Description:	Designed for either self-study or classroom use. Teaches all four language skills— speaking, listening (when used in conjunction with the audio), reading and writing . Offers clear, easy, step-by-step instruction building on what has been previously learned. Cassette tapes available. Paperback. 264 pages. 6" x 8.5"
Book	US$12.95 Stock # 1012
Three Tape Set	US$20.00 Stock # 1012T
Two CDs	US$20.00 Stock #1012CD

****

Title:	**Improving Your Thai Pronunciation**
Author:	Benjawan Poomsan Becker ©2003
Description:	Designed to help foreingers maximize their potential in pronouncing Thai words and enhance their Thai listening and speaking skills. Students will find that they have more confidence in speaking the language and can make themselves understood better. The book and the CDs are made to be used in combination. The course is straight forward , easy to follow and compact. Paperback. About 50 pages. 5" x 7.5" + One-hour CD
Book & CD	US$15.00 Stock # 1011

****

Deutschsprachiges Lehrbuch über die Thai-Sprache von Paiboon Publishing

Titel:	**Thai für Anfänger**
Autor:	Benjawan Poomsan Becker ©2000
Beschreibung:	Für das selbständige Lernen zu Hause oder für den Gebrauch im Klassenzimmer. Vermittelt Grundkenntnisse der Thai-Sprache. Das Buch kann mit den entsprechenden Tonbandkassetten kombiniert werden. Bietet klare und einfache Instruktionen, die Schritt für Schritt auf bereits Erlerntem aufbauen. Wird von zahlreichen Thai-Tempeln und Sprachinstituten in Amerika benutzt. Tonbandkassetten erhältlich. Taschenbuch. 245 Seiten. 15 cm x 22 cm

Buch	US$13.95	Lagernummer	1005
Kassetten (3er Set)	US$20.00	Lagernummer	1005T

****

All books are fun and easy to use.
Mit unseren Büchern macht das Lernen Spass.

PAIBOON PUBLISHING
ORDER FORM

QTY.	ITEM NO.	NAME OF ITEM	ITEM PRICE	TOTAL

Delivery Charges for First Class and Airmail

	USA and Canada	Other Countries
Up to $25.00	US$3.95	US$8.95
$25.01-$50.00	US$4.95	US$11.95
$50.01-$75.00	US$6.25	US$15.25
$75.01-$100.00	US$7.75	US$18.75
Over $100.00	FREE	US$18.75

Merchandise Total ____

CA residents add 8.25% sales tax

Delivery Charge (See Chart at Left) ____

Total ____

Method of Payment ❒ Check ❒ Money Order Make payable to Paiboon Publishing
Charge to: ❒ Visa ❒ Master Card

Card # _____ Exp. Date ____/____

Signature_____ Tel _____

Name _____ Date _____

Address _____

_____

_____

Email Address _____

Mail order is for orders outside of Thailand only.
Send your order and payment to: Paiboon Publishing
PMB 192, 1442A Walnut Street, Berkeley, CA 94709 USA
Tel: 1-510-848-7086 Fax: 1-510-848-4521
Email: orders@paiboonpublishing.com
Website: www.paiboonpublishing.com
Allow 2-3 weeks for delivery.

PAIBOON
PP
PUBLISHING

Printed by Chulalongkorn University Printing House
July, 2003   [4609-098/3,000(2)]
http://www.cuprint.chula.ac.th